CONTENTS

MADE TO BE BROKEN

THE 50 GREATEST RECORDS AND STREAKS IN SPORTS

ALLEN ST. JOHN

TRIUMPH
BOOKS
CHICAGO

For Margaret Barra, who'll do great things someday

Library of Congress Cataloging-in-Publication Data

St. John, Allen.
  Made to be broken : the 50 greatest records and streaks in sports /Allen St. John.
     p. cm.
  ISBN-13: 978-1-57243-857-6
  ISBN-10: 1-57243-857-6
  1. Sports records. 2. Sports—History. I. Title.
  GV741.S8 2006
  796.02'1—dc22
                         2006010711

This book is available in quantity at special discounts for your group or organization. For further information, contact:

Triumph Books
542 South Dearborn Street
Suite 750
Chicago, Illinois 60605
(312) 939-3330
Fax (312) 663-3557

Printed in U.S.A.

ISBN-13: 978-1-57243-857-6
ISBN-10: 1-57243-857-6

Design by Wagner Donovan Design

All photos courtesy of AP/Wide World Photos unless otherwise indicated

ACKNOWLEDGMENTS

First and foremost, my deepest thanks to my posse of crack researchers who helped shape this book as well as fill in the details that bring it to life. Matt Shepatin, research editor at *Playboy*, unearthed all sorts of amazing details, from the strange tale of Earl Webb to Mark Spitz's put-up-or-shut-up moment in Munich. Brian Lawshe will someday be as good a writer and editor as he is a golfer—if he isn't already. The incomparable James Martin of *Tennis* magazine has been my editor for years, and it was nice to have him feeding me information for a change. Gridiron guru Steve Silverman contributed to much of the hard-hitting football action in these pages.

Thanks to my pal Christopher Russo, my collaborator on the Mad Dog books and the best sports fan that I know. And my deepest gratitude to Paul Steiger, Eben Shapiro, Jeff Grocott, Steve Barnes, and all my friends at *The Wall Street Journal*.

And last but hardly least, all my love and gratitude to my wife, Sally, and my two children, Ethan and Emma. I'm your biggest fan.

INTRODUCTION

IN THE WORLD OF SPORTS, there are certain magic numbers that resonate with every fan: 755 homers, 100 points, 56 games, four minutes.

Why do these records loom so large in every sports fan's imagination? The first reason is that they answer the central question in the world of sports: who's the best? And a record answers it in a big way—a record isn't just about who's the best on any given afternoon, it's about who's the best of all time. It's the end point of achievement in a particular sport.

But the most important records aren't just numbers in a dusty record book. They represent a challenge to everyone who still plays the game. "Can you top this?" they seem to say.

But perhaps the most compelling thing about great records are the stories behind them. Stories of great athletes. Of great teams. Of great moments. Of milestones that have been reached and milestones that are still waiting to be passed.

Made to Be Broken is all about the magic in these numbers.

This book not only ranks the 50 greatest records in sports history, it brings these moments to life. It's an up-close-and-personal look at some of the most amazing feats in the world of sports and the all-time great athletes behind them.

Some are decades-long grinds like Hank Aaron's heroic pursuit of Babe Ruth's career home-run record. Others are lightning-in-a-bottle moments like Bob Beamon's Olympic long-jump record. Some are the result of a perfect storm of circumstance. Others are almost inexplicable. Some of these stories hearken all the way back to the Roaring Twenties, while others belong to players who can be seen on tomorrow night's edition of *SportsCenter*.

But what these records all share is a sense of possibility, the determination to push the envelope, the suspense of the chase, the thrill that comes with doing something that's never been done before. Faster. Higher. Longer. *Better.*

RANKING THE RECORDS

The records in this book run the gamut. Some are individual records, some represent team accomplishments. Some were set in less than a minute, some took more than 20 years. So how did I go about ranking these records? Because in many ways it's a task of comparing apples to oranges, crunching numbers doesn't yield final answers. The next best thing is to ask a few smart and pertinent questions about each record.

1. Is the record still on the books?

With a few exceptions, *Made to Be Broken* focuses on current records, marks that still stand.

2. Is it an undisputed record?

More often than you'd think, there's some controversy about which record is the legitimate mark. Do you discount a mark like Nap Lajoie's batting mark because it was set in the very first year of American League play? If it's a college record—like coaching wins in football and basketball—do you ignore marks set outside of Division 1-A? If it's not clear exactly who holds it, that affects the record's stature.

3. How long has it lasted?

A record that gets broken again and again—some swimming world records will fall several times in a season—must rank behind those records that have stood for years, decades, or even generations. One of my favorite examples is Rickey Henderson's runs-scored record. It was set by Ty Cobb in the mid-1920s and wasn't broken until 2001, which means that it withstood attacks from most of the game's greatest players: Ruth, Williams, DiMaggio, Musial, Mantle, Mays, and Aaron.

4. Does it represent a great afternoon? Or a great career?

In general, career records, which represent sustained excellence over a decade or more, get the nod over single-season marks. That's why Earl Webb slots in behind Pete Rose. Similarly, single-season marks generally take precedence over single-game marks. That's why you won't find, say, the most homers in a game or the most touchdowns in a half in this book.

5. Who set it?

Is the record holder a Hall of Famer? Is he one of the greatest players in the history of his sport? Or is he more of a one-dimensional player—yes, we're talking about you, Pete Rose—who's relatively ordinary in other aspects of the game?

6. Does it show up in the won-loss column?

There are a few records where there's a strange disconnect between remarkable statistical feats and winning and losing. Nolan Ryan's strikeouts. Dan Marino's yardage. And most notably Cal Ripken's consecutive-games streak, a record that probably cost his team victories.

7. Can it still be broken?

Certain marks, like the single-season record for triples and any number of pitching marks set in the early part of the 20th century, are a product of the way the game was played at the time. It's important to remember that the pendulum does swing back—Ty Cobb's stolen-base records seemed unapproachable for years, but if a modern player needs a time machine to challenge it, that pushes the record down the list some.

8. Is the record memorable?

Does the average sports fan know who holds the record, when it was set, and who held it before? This is kind of an X factor. Certain marks have captured the attention of the American public and jumped from the sports section to the front page. That's why Roger Bannister is on this list and Hicham El Guerrouj isn't, and why Mark Spitz is ahead of Larissa Latynina.

Now there's no record that hits all of these criteria, but every one in this book qualifies under at least one of these standards.

And, of course, my list is only the beginning. Read the book, watch the DVD, and then rank the records yourself.

#1

THE NEW SULTAN OF SWAT

WHEN HANK AARON PASSED BABE RUTH, HE SET THE GREATEST RECORD IN SPORTS

Hammerin' Hank, with wife Billye at his side, addresses the media after his historic 715th home run.

IT WAS BASEBALL'S GREAT ACHIEVEMENT, but hardly its greatest moment. Hank Aaron, the All-Star outfielder, spent most of his career hitting home runs quietly, in small-market cities like Milwaukee and Atlanta, overshadowed by contemporaries like Willie Mays and Mickey Mantle.

But as he neared Babe Ruth's career home-run record, once thought unapproachable, Aaron got noticed; he began receiving vicious, racist hate mail. The FBI was called in to deal with the death threats he was receiving almost daily, while his college-age daughter was the target of a kidnapping threat. "That will never be thrown away," Aaron said, of the reams of hate mail. "That wasn't long ago. We still have hatred in this country. We still have to be reminded that things are not as good as we think they are."

And even the commissioner interfered with Aaron's record run. Because he entered the 1974 season with 713, one short of Ruth's total, the Braves planned to sit Aaron during the opening series in Cincinnati so he could break the record at home. When Commissioner Bowie Kuhn became aware of this, he ordered the Braves to play Aaron in at least two of the first three away games. This made baseball history because while commissioners often told teams which player couldn't play—because of a suspension—this marked the only time in baseball history that a commissioner had ever told a team who they had to

> "THERE'S A DRIVE INTO LEFT-CENTER FIELD. THAT BALL IS GONNA BE…OUTTA HERE! IT'S GONE! IT'S 715! THERE'S A NEW HOME-RUN CHAMPION OF ALL TIME! AND IT'S HENRY AARON!"
> — BROADCASTER MILO HAMILTON'S HISTORIC CALL ON APRIL 8, 1974

IN IT FOR THE LONG HAUL

Aaron's remarkable achievement was due, in large part, to his incredible consistency and durability. He never hit more than 47 home runs in a single season, but he surpassed the 30-homer mark 15 times in his 23-year career and topped 40 eight times, including in 1973 at the age of 39.

put on the field. When Aaron did hit his record-breaking home run, Kuhn was not in attendance.

On Opening Day, April 4, 1974, six years to the day after Martin Luther King Jr. was assassinated, Aaron hit a three-run homer off Jack Billingham, to tie Babe Ruth's record, with his 714th home run. The number had such resonance that Jack Webb wore 714 as his badge number in Dragnet as homage to Ruth. Aaron didn't play the second game and went 0 for 3 in the last game of the three-game series.

On Monday, April 8, the Braves' first game back in Atlanta, Aaron walked in the second inning and came around to score his 2,063rd run, setting a new National League record. In the fourth, he crushed an Al Downing pitch into the left-field bullpen. Announcer Milo Hamilton had the historic call.

"He's sitting on 714. Here's the pitch by Downing…swinging…There's a drive into left-center field. That ball is gonna be…outta here! It's gone! It's 715! There's a new home-run champion of all time! And it's Henry Aaron!"

The ball flew into the left-field bullpen, where it was caught by relief pitcher Tom House. "If I had stood perfectly still, the ball would have hit me in the forehead," House recalled.

What should have been one of the game's great moments, a great record broken by a player whose hallmark was his quiet dignity, instead became a kind of anticlimax. "Thank God it's over," said the

last active former Negro Leaguer after breaking the record.

It's fitting that Aaron broke the record in Atlanta. Just as Ruth benefited from the short right-field porch in Yankee Stadium, Aaron had some help from his surroundings. His remarkable home run totals while in his mid- to late 30s were a result of the Braves' move from Milwaukee, which was a relatively neutral home-run park, to Atlanta Fulton County Stadium, which was nicknamed the "Launching Pad." Half of his eight 40-homer campaigns came in Atlanta, including one only four months shy of his 40th birthday. The higher home-run totals in Atlanta weren't attributable to the stadium's dimensions, which were quite average, but to the altitude, which at the time was the highest of any major league city.

Aaron would return to Milwaukee to play for the Brewers and end his career where he started it. On July 20, 1976, against Dick Drago of the Angels, Aaron hit the 755th and last home run of his career.

Aaron's record has endured quietly, like the man who set it, and it's stood for longer than Ruth's record. During the hitting craze of the mid-1990s any number of players were on pace to shatter the record. But one by one the contenders—Ken Griffey Jr., Juan Gonzalez, Frank Thomas—were derailed by injury. Older contenders like Mark McGwire and Sammy Sosa also ended their playing days before even approaching Aaron's record. The only other player to pass Ruth,

Atlanta Braves slugger Hank Aaron breaks Babe Ruth's record for career home runs with number 715 off of Dodgers pitcher Al Downing on April 8, 1974.

Barry Bonds, will likely end his career before catching Aaron. Older contenders like Mark McGuire and Sammy Sosa also ended their playing days before even approaching Aaron's record. The only other player to pass Ruth, Barry Bonds will likely have to play until 2007 and beyond to catch Aaron, and the controversy surrounding his alleged use of performance-enhancing drugs will taint his record bid in the eyes of many fans.

More than three decades after setting it, Aaron summed up the appeal of his timeless record. "The fans don't care about watching a no-hitter or a one-hitter. They want to see runs scored, people circling the bases, balls flying out of the ballpark. Anytime baseball is in trouble, they bring the home run back," said Aaron. "A home run is the greatest thing in sports." And no one in major league history hit more of them than the great Henry Aaron.

MY OH MY

Of course, Aaron's record has been broken once already—by a Japanese player. The legendary Sadaharu Oh of the Yomiuri Giants broke Aaron's mark by hitting his 756th home run on September 3, 1977. Oh's career high was 55 homers in 140 games. Oh, who practiced samurai swordsmanship as a way to help him hit the curve ball, retired with a world record 856 round-trippers.

2

CATCH AS CATCH CAN

JERRY RICE'S CAREER TD MARK IS THE MOST ENDURING OF HIS MANY NFL RECORDS

The Most Valuable Player of Super Bowl XXIII gives the Lombardi Trophy a kiss after defeating the Bengals 20–16 on January 22, 1989.

WHO HOLDS THE RECORD FOR HOLDING records in professional football? That would be wide receiver Jerry Rice, whose name can be found atop a mind-boggling 38 lists in the NFL record book.

So picking a single mark from that bunch can be a chore in itself, but if he had to choose, Rice would probably pick the touchdown mark as his favorite.

First off, the old record holder was his idol, Steve Largent. Rice wore No. 80 in Largent's honor and kept a Wheaties box with Largent's picture on the cover in his locker. Largent's record was also one of those nice round numbers in the world of sports—100. But finally, and most importantly, the whole object of the game of football is to get the ball into the end zone. And that's what Jerry Rice did more often than any other player in football history.

The 13-time Pro Bowler almost doubled Largent's old record, catching 197 scoring passes. He also rushed for 10 touchdowns and added one TD return for an all-time record of 208. And even though touchdown catches are far rarer than touchdown runs are, Rice tops all running backs in scoring

as well, with Emmitt Smith coming closest with 175 TDs. But when it comes to scoring efficiency, there's no contest. Rice scored a TD every 7.86 times he touched the ball, compared with every 28.13 times for Smith.

Rice's most amazing year was 1987, in which he scored a single-season record 22 touchdown catches, far eclipsing Mark Clayton's old mark of 18. But what makes Rice's record truly special is that 1987 was a strike year, and Rice accomplished this in only 12 games. Oh, and he also added a rushing touchdown for good measure.

To get a measure of just how good Rice really was, let's turn to that record book again. Cris Carter is second behind Rice with 130 receiving TDs. That's a gap of 67 scores. That's the same as the gap between Carter and Terance Mathis, Anthony Miller, Carl Pickens, and John Stallworth, who are tied for 44th place on the touchdown list with 63. Yes, 44th place. It's the same with receiving yards. Rice is at 22,895. Tim Brown is 7,961 yards behind in second with 14,934. Given this amazing superiority, it's reasonable to argue that Rice

CRIS CARTER IS SECOND BEHIND RICE WITH 131 RECEIVING TDS. THAT'S A GAP OF 67 SCORES. THAT'S THE SAME AS THE GAP BETWEEN CARTER AND TERANCE MATHIS, ANTHONY MILLER, CARL PICKENS, AND JOHN STALLWORTH, WHO ARE ALL TIED FOR 44TH PLACE ON THE TOUCHDOWN LIST WITH 63. YES, 44TH PLACE.

Rice shows the athleticism and concentration that made him the NFL's all-time leading touchdown scorer, hauling in this pass despite having defender Ray Buchanan's hand firmly planted in his facemask.

JERRY'S CLUTCH CATCHES

In the postseason Rice was especially super. He holds post-season records for games played (28), touchdowns (22), catches (151), receiving yards (2,245), and consecutive games with at least one reception (274). He also holds Super Bowl records for receptions (33), receiving yards (589), all-purpose yards (604), and points (48).

Jerry Rice breaks free from the grip of Atlanta's Juran Bolden during the 1998 season for one of his 207 career touch-downs, a 26-yard reception from 49ers quarterback Steve Young.

is not only the greatest receiver in pro football history, but the best player.

While Rice's records are amazing, they may not be unbreakable. The NFL is becoming more and more of a passing league, and Randy Moss, for one, who had 98 TDs and more than 10,000 receiving yards entering the 2006 season, is actually ahead of Rice's record pace. This may be what kept Rice in the game, moving from the Raiders to the Seahawks to the Broncos, piling up yards and catching touch-downs until well into his forties.

CAUGHT IN THE DRAFT

Jerry Rice not only kept defensive coordinators up at night, but general managers, too. The greatest receiver of all time was hardly a can't-miss prospect. When he was drafted in 1985, teams focused on his lack of speed—he only ran a 4.6 in the 40-yard dash—and the fact that while he put up huge numbers, averaging 10 catches a game, he did so for tiny Mississippi Valley State. That's why he slipped to 16th in the draft and was the third receiver selected, picked behind Al Toon at 10 and Eddie Brown at 13.

THE GREATEST ONE

WAYNE GRETZKY OWNS THE NHL RECORD BOOK, BUT HIS POINTS-SCORED MARK IS THE MOST MAJESTIC OF ALL

WAYNE GRETZKY COLLECTED 1,963 ASSISTS during regular-season games. It's a big number, to be sure, but just how big?

Let's put this record in some perspective. The legendary Gordie Howe, who was hockey's all-time leading scorer before Gretzky came along, had 1,850 points in his career, which means that if Wayne Gretzky had never scored a single goal (and he scored an NHL-record 894) he would still be the greatest scorer in hockey history. To look at it another way, it took Gretzky only 681 games to break Howe's record of 1,049 assists. That's 1,086 games—or 13 seasons—fewer than it took Gordie. Another comparison: Gretzky has more assists than Hall of Famers Bobby Orr (645), Henri Richard (688), and Mike Bossy (553) put together.

Wayne Gretzky, virtual owner of the NHL's record books, skates for the Edmonton Oilers during the 1985 season. His 1,963 career regular-season assists is probably the most astonishing feat on his resume. Photo courtesy of Getty Images.

The greatest hockey player of all time retired as a New York Ranger on April 18, 1999.

But the career-assists record is merely the most remarkable entry in Wayne Gretzky's remarkable resume. Midway through the 2006 season, Gretzky held or tied a startling total of 61 records: 40 for the regular season, 15 for the playoffs, and another six for the All-Star game. He set the single-season record for goals with 92, demolishing Phil Esposito's old record of 76. He is the only player to score 200 points, and he did it three times, including his record of 215 in 1985–86. But it was assists that really set The Great One apart. In only his second year, Gretzky broke the NHL record with 109 assists, becoming only the second player, after Bobby Orr, to reach triple digits in assists.

He would notch 100 assists an astonishing 11 times in a row. He owns the seven best single-season assist marks, including his record of 163 in 1985–1986, when he averaged more than two assists per game. Gretzky was hockey's answer to Babe Ruth—a player who rewrote the record book, changed the game, and dazzled fans and opponents alike.

"Trying to stop Wayne is like throwing a blanket over a ghost," said Los Angeles Kings coach Parker McDonald. Gretzky broke Howe's career-assist record on March 1, 1988, against the Kings, and it was vintage Gretzky. The Great One camped out behind the net. He saw teammate Jarri Kurri put it on his stick, and history was made. Even some of the reporters covering the game didn't see it, because they were still writing down the details of the goal Gretzky had scored only 18 seconds earlier.

And it was a low-key affair. Gretzky's wife, Janet Jones, was out of town doing an audition; Oilers

> "**T**RYING TO STOP **W**AYNE IS LIKE
> THROWING A BLANKET OVER A GHOST."
> —L.A. K**INGS COACH** P**ARKER** M**C**D**ONALD**

owner Peter Pocklington missed the moment because his flight was delayed; NHL president John Zeigler stayed in New York for league meetings; and the record holder, Gordie Howe, called Gretzky as he neared the record and The Great One assured Howe that there was no need to rearrange his schedule to be there when the mark fell.

The record-breaking assist also came at the very end of Gretzky's tenure with the Edmonton Oilers (he would be traded to the Kings the following autumn). On the day that he broke the record, Gretzky was asked how many he might end up with. "It would be nice to get to 1,500," he said. "I don't think that would be unreasonable to ask for me to get there."

His estimate was off by only 463 points, which would be four very good seasons for any other NHL star. "He's a genius," says goalie Mike Liut. "I'd see him come down the ice and immediately start thinking, 'What don't I see that Wayne's seeing right now?'"

More often than anyone in NHL history, it was a teammate in a position to score.

DON'T TOUCH MY STICK

The Great One is superstitious about his equipment. "I don't like my hockey sticks touching other sticks, and I don't like them crossing one another. I put baby powder on the ends. I think it's essentially a matter of taking care of what takes care of you."

STILL SUPER MARIO

If Wayne Gretzky had never existed, Mario Lemieux might be considered the greatest player in hockey history. He trails only Gretzky in single-season points (199), assists (114), and assists per game; goals per game and points per game; and he owns the second-longest point-scoring streak (46 games). His 85 goals in 1988–89 trail only Gretzky and Brett Hull. Mario's only major regular-season record? Most shorthanded goals in a season, 13, in 1988–1989.

For the sensational Mario Lemieux, second best will have to do, at least in the record books.

4

THE STREAK

JOE DIMAGGIO'S 56-GAME HITTING STREAK HAS BECOME AS
LEGENDARY AS THE PLAYER WHO SET IT

ONE OF BASEBALL'S GREATEST RECORDS
began not with a bang, but a dribbler. Facing Ed Smith
of the Chicago White Sox on May 15, 1941, the New
York Yankees' Joe DiMaggio was not worried about
streaks but simply wanted to get on base when he
managed a weak single. But on that day, with one hit
in four at-bats, Joltin' Joe began a 56-game stretch of
near perfection.

"Baseball didn't really get into my blood until I
knocked off that hitting streak," DiMaggio recalled.
"Getting a daily hit became more important to me
than eating, drinking, or sleeping."

In the 1940s, hitting streaks weren't a big deal,
but if anyone had forecast a player to piece a long one
together, the Yankee Clipper would have been a solid
choice. While in the Pacific Coast League, DiMaggio
had once hit in an amazing 61 consecutive games.
And in the spring training of 1941, DiMaggio had not
gone a single exhibition game without at least a single.

However, the season didn't begin so well.
DiMaggio, the two-time defending American League
batting champ, was struggling at the plate, and his
average was below .300. But after the scratch single
against the Sox, DiMaggio turned things around in
dramatic fashion. As the hits began to pile up, the
New York sportswriters, who rarely paid attention to
hitting streaks, began to dust off old record books to

put DiMaggio's streak in perspective. It was discovered
that Wee Willie Keeler of the Baltimore Orioles held
the major league record at 44 games, while George
Sisler had set the AL mark in 1922 with 41 straight
games with a hit.

But as DiMaggio marched toward immortality,
there were close calls aplenty. In fact, of the 56 games
in the streak, he managed only one base hit in 34
of them.

On June 17, 1941, DiMaggio was still two
games short of Rogers Hornsby's record for a right-
handed hitter—32 games—when he faced Chicago's
Johnny Rigney. Late in the game, DiMaggio hit what
looked like a routine grounder at shortstop Luke
Appling, but the ball took an erratic bounce, and
Appling was unable to throw him out. Then the
very next day, DiMaggio again hit a ball at Appling,
but this time it was a bullet, and the future Hall of

JOE D PLUS TWO

While playing at Oklahoma State University between
1985 and 1988, future Major Leaguer Robin Ventura
hit in 58 consecutive games, the longest hitting
steak in college baseball history.

Famer could only knock it down. Both were ruled hits by official scorer Dan Daniel, the only ones he managed either day.

On June 29, DiMaggio tied Sisler's record in the first game of a doubleheader with the Washington Senators and broke it in the nightcap, tallying a single hit in each game. However, an overzealous fan had swiped the Clipper's favorite piece of lumber while no one was watching, visibly upsetting the normally stoic DiMaggio. It didn't make any difference, though. Borrowing an identical bat from teammate Tommy Henrich, Joltin' Joe hammered out hits in the next three games to surpass Keeler. Luck was on his side in game number 44 when he

Joe DiMaggio lines a single to left field on June 29, 1941, to extend his hitting streak to an American League–record 42 games, breaking the 19-year-old mark previously held by George Sisler.

In the years since, no player has gotten within a dozen games of DiMaggio's mark, with Pete Rose coming closest with a 44-game streak. Baseball analyst Bill James decided to find out just how singular DiMaggio's streak was. He programmed a simulation game with DiMaggio's career stats and then set it to play 1,000 seasons. Not once during that time did the Virtual Clipper hit in 56 games in a row.

DiMaggio and Ted Williams (left) teamed up in the 1941 All-Star game. Despite hitting .406 that season, Williams finished second to Joltin' Joe in the '41 MVP balloting.

got on base early, because the game was called after the fifth inning. The record breaker in game number 45 came on a tape-measure blast off the Red Sox's 19-game winner Dick Newsome. Then, with the pressure reduced, DiMaggio got really hot, hitting .575 in games 47–56.

In game 57 against the Cleveland Indians, however, Joe's luck ran out. It wasn't really the pitching that caught up with him—he hit a pair of bullets down the third-base line. But third sacker Ken Keltner made two brilliant plays to halt the record-setting streak of 56 games.

DiMaggio spent little time mourning the end of the streak, as he promptly began a 16-game streak the next day to finish with hits in 72 out of 73 games while leading the Yanks to a pennant. That year, even though his rival Ted Williams hit .406, the Yankee Clipper was named the AL's Most Valuable Player.

"BASEBALL DIDN'T REALLY GET INTO MY BLOOD UNTIL I KNOCKED OFF THAT HITTING STREAK. GETTING A DAILY HIT BECAME MORE IMPORTANT TO ME THAN EATING, DRINKING, OR SLEEPING."

—JOE DIMAGGIO

5

THE KEY TO 88

JOHN WOODEN LED UCLA TO AN UNFATHOMABLE STRING OF REGULAR-SEASON VICTORIES

UCLA coach John Wooden holds the trophy while forward Sidney Wicks wears the net following the Bruins' NCAA championship-game victory on March 27, 1971, early in their 88-game winning streak, which had begun two months earlier.

IF ONLY EVERY GREAT STREAK HAD SUCH perfect symmetry. UCLA's record 88-game winning streak began on January 30, 1971, a week after losing to Notre Dame in South Bend 89–82. Three years later to the month, the streak would end in the very same arena with the Irish defeating UCLA 71–70.

During the streak, the Bruins claimed three national titles in the process and earned All-America honors for four different players. Thanks to freshman eligibility rules preventing anyone from playing that many seasons, none of the Bruins participated throughout the entire streak. Larry Farmer and Larry Hollyfield were around for 75 of those victories.

"Any streak of that sort is remarkable in any sport at any level," Wooden says. "A lot of things have to fall into place. You have to have a little luck." The largest margin of victory during the streak was against Texas A&M on December 11, 1971, the Bruins winning by a score of 117–53, the fourth-largest margin in UCLA history. The next week they went on to defeat Notre Dame almost as badly, 114–53. Three of the school's top-10 largest margins of victory were set in 1971. The next week they would record their highest point total during the streak with a 119–81 victory over Texas Christian. The lowest score for an opponent during the streak

LEGEND OF THE RUBBER MAN

John Wooden is one of only three individuals (Lenny Wilkens and Bill Sharman are the others) to be inducted into the Basketball Hall of Fame as both a player and a coach. Wooden was a three-time All-American guard at Purdue between 1928 and 1934, where he was known as the "Indiana Rubber Man."

was 32 by Notre Dame on January 29, 1972. There were no overtime games during the streak.

But it wasn't always that easy. Perhaps the Bruins' toughest battle came on February 6, 1971, just two games into the streak, when UCLA traveled to the Sports Arena to face off against conference rival USC. The Bruins came back from nine points down in the second half for a 64–60 triumph. They traveled north for their next two games, surviving close calls against Oregon (69–68) and Oregon State (67–65).

The 1972–1973 season, on the other hand, was a little less nerve-wracking, as the Bruins won every game by at least six points and 23 of 26 by a double-digit margin. The only time UCLA ever had back-to-back perfect records for a full season was during the streak, going 30–0 in 1972 and 1973.

On January 27, 1973, UCLA broke the existing consecutive-game record, a 60-game winning streak, set by Bill Russell's University of San Francisco team. The Bruins won their 61st game against Notre Dame, 82–63. Bill Walton led the way with 16 points, 15 rebounds, and 10 blocked shots. Wooden said it was "just another game." He continued: "This isn't the greatest thing that happened on this day. It is my granddaughter's birthday, too. But the most important thing is that this was cease-fire day in Vietnam. That's much more important than this."

The streak ended almost a year later on January 18, 1974, with a 71–70 loss to Notre Dame. In that game, the Irish had trailed 70–59 with 3:32 but outscored the Bruins 12–0 down the stretch to win by one point. It was the first time senior Walton had suffered a defeat as a varsity player. The young coach of the Notre Dame team that ended the streak was none other than Digger Phelps.

"This is the greatest thing that could happen for collegiate basketball," said Phelps of the winning streak's end.

"I honestly have no feelings either way about our winning streak being ended," said Wooden. "I've said at least 100 times that once we broke the record for consecutive victories, the length of the streak was meaningless. The important thing was breaking the consecutive record."

Wooden was asked if he could vote UCLA number-one in that week's coaches' poll. "No," he said, "I can't." Who will you vote for, then? "For Notre Dame, of course," he replied. The Bruins did lose their number-one rank but regained the top spot one week later by crushing Notre Dame at home 94–75.

Was it a relief to have the streak end? "Yes, that's true," he said. "It was a relief because it was beginning to affect the players. Once we got into the 80s, people started talking about 100. We were able to relax more after that."

Relaxed or not, the Bruins ended the season on a sour note. In the semifinal game of the Final Four, they ran up against a David Thompson–led North Carolina State squad. The game went into double overtime, and the Bruins built a seven-point lead during the second extra session, but the Wolfpack clawed back and won 80–77. That ended a winning streak in some ways more impressive—38 games without a defeat in the NCAA tournament—a streak that began in 1964 and accounted for nine national titles.

Wooden addresses his team in the closing moments of the game that would end the streak, a 71–70 loss to Notre Dame in which the Bruins had the ball after this timeout but failed to score.

COVER BOYS

During the streak, UCLA basketball players and coaches appeared on the cover of *Sports Illustrated* an astonishing 12 times. Bill Walton led the club with five appearances, followed by Lew Alcindor (four times total, once as Kareem), Steve Patterson (once), Gail Goodrich (once), and head coach John Wooden (once). So much for the cover jinx.

COMING HOME

RICKEY HENDERSON CIRCLED THE BASES
MORE OFTEN THAN ANY PLAYER IN BASEBALL HISTORY

EVERY BASEBALL PLAYER HAS ONE ULTIMATE goal when he steps up to the plate. Touching them all. Circling the bases. Coming home. Scoring. It's an equal-opportunity desire, one that applies equally to the lumbering slugger and the speediest leadoff man. Who has put a digit up on the scoreboard more often than any player in baseball history?

Rickey Henley Henderson. Henderson is best known for his stolen-base exploits, but in 2001 he broke one of the longest-standing and most important records in baseball. In an October 4 game against the Dodgers, Henderson hit a home run to score the 2,246th run of his career and make history.

The career runs-scored mark of 2,245 was held by Ty Cobb, and while it didn't get quite the attention of some other records, it stayed on the books longer than just about any major offensive mark. Babe Ruth, Lou Gehrig, Joe DiMaggio, Ted Williams, Willie Mays, Mickey Mantle, Hank Aaron, and every other great hitter in history aimed for Cobb's record and fell short. Until Henderson.

Henderson's record-breaking moment was hardly big news. The headlines in September 2001 were, of course, dominated by world and national events. On the sports page, the biggest baseball news was Barry Bonds's pursuit of the single-season home run record (he hit his 70th home run the day that Henderson passed Cobb) and the impending retirement of Cal Ripken and Henderson's teammate Tony Gwynn (Henderson collected his 3,000th hit in Gwynn's last game).

That's typical of Henderson, perhaps the game's most underrated superstar. His career batting average of .279 isn't extraordinary. But what made him a run-scoring machine was his ability to get on base, as evidenced by his career .401 on-base percentage, which is higher than that of Joe DiMaggio, Willie Mays, Honus Wagner, and Rod Carew. His severely crouched batting stance gave pitchers a small target and, coupled with his sharp batting eye, made Henderson one of the toughest players in baseball to pitch to.

Henderson broke the career record for walks previously held by Babe Ruth. Henderson, the greatest base stealer of all time, seems to be the last person any pitcher would want to put on base. Still, by contrast, the portly Ruth did relatively little damage on the base paths. In Game 7 of the 1926 World Series, up by a run in the ninth inning, Grover Cleveland Alexander walked Ruth, who was thrown out trying to steal second for the final out of the series. Henderson ended his career with a remarkable 2,190 bases on balls, a record since surpassed by Barry Bonds.

There were, of course, plenty of instances where Henderson scored without any additional help. He

Henderson retreats back to first base after Devil Rays pitcher Julio Santana gave him a second look during a 1998 game.

BAND ON THE RUN

The runs-scored record has one of the cleanest progressions in baseball history. Ross Barnes of the Boston Red Stockings took possession of the record with 66 runs scored in 31 games back in 1871. Jim O'Rourke broke the record in 1882 and finished his career with 1,728 runs scored. Cap Anson topped it in 1894 and finished with 1,996 runs, a record that stood until Cobb captured it in 1925.

hit 297 career home runs—more than Roger Maris—and holds the major league record with 81 career leadoff homers.

It's this combination of assets—patience, power, and speed on the bases—that made Henderson the greatest leadoff hitter of all time and gave him one of the game's most coveted records. "When I was asked the question, 'What's the most important thing for you to do?' I always said, 'Scoring runs,'" Henderson explained as he chased Cobb. "A leadoff hitter's job is to come across the plate." And no one did that more often than Rickey Henderson.

"WHEN I WAS ASKED THE QUESTION, 'WHAT'S THE MOST IMPORTANT THING FOR YOU TO DO?' I ALWAYS SAID SCORING RUNS. A LEADOFF HITTER'S JOB IS TO COME ACROSS THE PLATE."

—RICKEY HENDERSON

Rickey Henderson points toward Padres teammates waiting at home plate to celebrate his record-setting 2,246th career run scored on October 4, 2001. Henderson broke Ty Cobb's long-standing record with this solo home run in a game against the Dodgers.

7

THE GAME OF THE CENTURY

WILT CHAMBERLAIN'S 100-POINT GAME WAS A PERFORMANCE FOR THE AGES

Wilt Chamberlain holds up a sign signifying his historic night in Hershey, Pennsylvania, on March 2, 1962, when he scored 100 points against the New York Knicks.

"IT CAN'T HAPPEN AGAIN." That's what Michael Jordan said about Wilt Chamberlain's 100-point night, back in 1990. "A team simply wouldn't let you score that many. Not even close to it." Now, whether 81 points is close or not is debatable, but Chamberlain's 44-year-old record has never been seriously challenged.

Chamberlain drops in his last basket of the evening, giving him an even 100 for the game against a stunned New York Knicks team and an awestruck crowd in Hershey, Pennsylvania.

The date was March 2, 1962, and the game between the Knicks and the Philadelphia Warriors was played at an almost neutral site, at the Hershey Sports Arena in Hershey, Pennsylvania. Wilt's Warriors charged out to a 19–3 lead. By the end of the first quarter, Philadelphia had outscored New York 42–26 with Wilt accounting for 23 of his team's 42 points.

Chamberlain had 18 points in the second quarter, and a total of 41 points by halftime. He was 14 of 26 from the field and an unusually strong 13 of 14 from the charity stripe. "I wasn't thinking of hitting 100 but after putting in nine straight free throws I was thinking about a foul-shooting record," Wilt recalled. "It was my greatest game."

In the third quarter, Chamberlain scored 28 points, including a perfect 8 for 8 from the line.

Going into the final quarter, Wilt had 69 points, and began to think that he might be able to break his own record—78 points scored against the Lakers the previous December.

After he scored three quick baskets in the fourth, the crowd began chanting, "Give it to Wilt! Give it to Wilt!" Wilt still needed 11 points with five minutes to go, and the Knicks gave up hope of winning the game and concentrated on stopping Wilt, often holding the ball instead of going for the quick score, and forcing the Warriors to foul in order to conserve time despite their big lead.

"Those last three or four minutes were frantic," said Warriors forward Tom Meschery. "The Knicks were running around like chickens with their heads cut off, trying to foul anyone but Wilt. We started inbounding the ball straight to Wilt in the frontcourt."

The Big Dipper was still one basket short with 1:27 left on the clock. Wilt missed a shot, rebounded it, and missed again. Ted Luckenbill grabbed the rebound and passed to Joe Ruklick. Ruklick fed Wilt underneath the basket, and Chamberlain had his 100th point. "Wilt just carried people with him and did his power dunk," said Luckenbill. "That was all she wrote."

Or was it a dunk? Some say number 100 was a jump shot. No one seems to know for sure because video of the game does not exist. The game wasn't televised, and the only account is the radio play-by-play done by Bill Campbell. And not many saw history made in person. The official crowd was listed at 4,124. "I guess I've heard 40,000 people claim to have been there that night," said Harvey Pollack, the official statistician. "But the building was only about half full."

> "THOSE LAST THREE OR FOUR MINUTES WERE FRANTIC. THE KNICKS WERE RUNNING AROUND LIKE CHICKENS WITH THEIR HEADS CUT OFF, TRYING TO FOUL ANYONE BUT WILT. WE STARTED INBOUNDING THE BALL STRAIGHT TO WILT IN THE FRONTCOURT."
>
> —WARRIORS FORWARD TOM MESCHERY

The record-breaking basket was scored with 46 seconds left on the clock, but because fans stormed the court and the players had no desire to continue, the game ended prematurely. The game ball was taken out of play and signed after Wilt made his 100 but nobody knows what happened to it. The final score was 169–147, with the Knicks setting a record that night for most points by a losing team.

Wilt shot 36 for 63 from the field, setting records for both field goals made and field goals attempted. But the real key to the milestone was this: Chamberlain, who was a 51 percent career free-throw shooter, made 28 out of 32 from the line. "That almost makes me as happy as the 100," he said.

The only player to even approach his record is Kobe Bryant, who scored 81 points in January of 2006. Interestingly, Bryant actually scored a higher percentage of his team's points (81 of 120, or 67.5 percent) than did Chamberlain (100 of 169, or 59.2 percent). Chamberlain owns the next two spots on the highest-scoring list. He scored 78 against the Lakers in Philadelphia on December 8, 1961, in a triple OT game, breaking Elgin Baylor's record of 71 points. Asked if he was upset about losing the record that way Baylor replied presciently, "No, one day that guy's going to score 100." Chamberlain also had 73 points in regulation against Chicago on January 13, 1962, and 73 against New York on November 16, 1962. Nugget David Thompson also scored 73 against Detroit on April 9, 1978.

The 100-point game was merely one of the highlights of a season for the ages. Chamberlain scored a record 4,029 points that season, and his 50.4 points per game were also a record. "You have to remember that I averaged 50 points a game that year," Chamberlain explained. "Players that average 16 or 17 points usually have at least one game during a season when they score 35. That's just what I did; I doubled my average."

MIKE VS. WILT

One of the closest scoring races in NBA history was atop the career-scoring charts, and Wilt Chamberlain ended up a very close second. At the time of Michael Jordan's second retirement—after the 1998 season—he was the NBA's all-time leading scorer by a substantial margin at 31.5 points per game. Jordan came back with the Wizards playing with reduced effectiveness, and his career scoring average fell with virtually every game. When he retired for good, his average was 30.12, just a hairsbreadth ahead of Wilt's 30.09. If he had played only a dozen more games at that level, Jordan would have slipped behind Chamberlain. Is it just a coincidence that Michael hung them up when he did? You be the judge.

8

WIN SONG

CY YOUNG'S RECORD FOR CAREER VICTORIES IS THE PRODUCT OF HISTORY—AND PURE GREATNESS

OLD DENTON TRUE YOUNG—CY, SHORT for Cyclone, to his friends—poses a bit of a conundrum for modern baseball fans. His 511 wins stand as perhaps the most singularly unbreakable career record in all of baseball. And most fans assume that this amazing record is as much a testament to the way the game has changed as it is to Young's excellence as a pitcher. That's only partly true.

Young was born in 1867, when Andrew Johnson was president, two years after the end of the Civil War. When he broke into the Major Leagues in 1890, baseball was an entirely different game. The four ball and foul strike rules were freshly minted and the distance from the mound to the plate was only 50' instead of the 60'6" of the contemporary game.

The state of the game did allow Young to pitch plenty. In his second full year, he started 49 times and won 36 games and almost repeated the feat the following season, with 46 starts and 34 wins. That's how Young ended up with 511 wins.

Appearing in an Old-Timers game in 1937, Young (left) poses with former outfielder and manager Tris Speaker.

To put Young's win total in some perspective, let's look at some contemporary pitchers. In 2005, Dontrelle Willis of the Marlins led the majors with 22 wins. To equal Young's win total, a pitcher would have to average 22 wins for more than 23 years, year in and year out from the time he's 21 until he's 44. Looked at another way, if you added Hall of Famer Tom Seaver's 311 wins to the 197 that Pedro Martinez had entering the 2006 season, you'd still be three wins shy.

That said, there's the perception that Cy Young is purely the product of an age in which pitchers pitched far more than they do today. That's not exactly the case. Sure, Young is the career leader with 815 starts, recording 40 or more starts in a season 11 times. But second is Nolan Ryan, not all that far behind with 773. And of the top 10 on that list, all but Young and Pud Galvin (eighth with 689) pitched their entire careers after 1960.

What was different is that Young almost always finished what he started, which meant that he invariably got the decision. He completed 749 of his 815 starts, a mind-boggling 91.9 percent. By contrast, Tom Seaver completed only 231 of his 647 starts (35.7 percent) and Roger Clemens, entering the 2006 season, completed only 118 of 671, a 17.6 percent rate.

Interestingly, the secret to Young's longevity may have been his lack of training. His off-season regimen consisted of manual labor, notably chopping wood by the cord. All year long, he left all his throwing for the game.

THE RIGHT CYs

The Cy Young Award was initiated in 1956 by commissioner Ford Frick in honor of the Hall of Famer who died a year earlier. For the first 11 years, the award honored the best pitcher in baseball. (Don Newcombe was the first winner in 1956.) In 1967, after Frick's retirement, it was expanded to honor the best pitcher in each league.

"When I would go to spring training, I would never touch a ball for three weeks," Young said. "I never did any unnecessary throwing. I figured the old arm had just so many throws in it, and there wasn't any use wasting them."

As the holder of a record that seems like an untouchable anachronism from a bygone era, Young is known mostly as the namesake of pitching's most prestigious award. Yes, it's true that modern innovations such as the four-man rotation and the rise of relief pitching have put Cy Young's record permanently out of reach for even today's best pitchers. But know this, too—for the first seven decades of the 20th century there were plenty of other pitchers who took the mound almost as often as Cy Young. And not a single one of them recorded 511 wins or anything close.

"WHEN I WOULD GO TO SPRING TRAINING, I WOULD NEVER TOUCH THE BALL FOR THREE WEEKS. I NEVER DID ANY UNNECESSARY THROWING. I FIGURED THE OLD ARM HAD JUST SO MANY THROWS IN IT, AND THERE WASN'T ANY USE WASTING THEM."
—CY YOUNG

THE *L* WORD

Who holds the record for most losses? In one of those classic trivia questions, it's also Cy Young, with 316. While his win mark is unapproachable, a few modern pitchers have come close to his loss mark.

1. Cy Young		316
2. Pud Galvin		310
3. Nolan Ryan		292
4. Walter Johnson		279
5. Phil Niekro		274
6. Gaylord Perry		265
7. Don Sutton		256
8. Jack Powell		254
9. Eppa Rixey		251
10. Bert Blyleven		250

Cy Young, baseball's most winning and most prolific pitcher, throws for the Cleveland Indians in this undated photo taken around the turn of the century.

9 A LEAP OF FAITH

BOB BEAMON SHOCKED THE WORLD—AND HIMSELF— WITH HIS RECORD LONG JUMP

THERE IS MUCH TO BE SAID FOR THE quiet satisfaction of watching an athlete close in on a career record, inching closer, day by day, to a goal that's months or even years away. But in terms of sheer excitement, there is little to match those moments when, in an instant, an athlete redefines our concept of what's possible, shocking the world and himself. The ultimate lightning-in-a-bottle

Bob Beamon lands during his world-record-setting long jump at the 1968 Mexico City Olympic Games, astonishing observers, himself, and the other competitors.

moment was Bob Beamon's world-record long jump in the 1968 Olympics.

While history has made Beamon seem like the ultimate one-hit wonder, the backstory was a little different. He had a great season in 1968 and entered the Olympics as the favorite for the gold medal, even though he would be competing against the jumpers who shared the world record—Igor Ter-Ovanesyan of the Soviet Union and his American teammate Ralph Boston. On the one hand, Beamon won 22 of 23 events coming into Mexico City. On the other, Beamon was without a coach, since he was suspended by the University of Texas–El Paso because he refused to compete against Brigham Young University in protest of the school's racial policies. None of this could prepare anyone for what was to come.

Beamon came within a hairsbreadth of missing his date with history. In the qualifying rounds he fouled on his first two attempts. One more miscue and his Olympics would be history. Boston took him aside and suggested that he modify his approach and launch from well behind the board. Beamon took the advice and qualified easily for the finals.

His first jump in the finals was one of the most amazing moments in sports. Beamon's low-earth orbit landed so far down the pit that he outsailed the range of the new optical measurement system. Judges came up with an old-school steel tape and put the number up on the board: 8.90 meters. Beamon knew he had uncorked an amazing jump, but he didn't understand the implications of what he had done until he saw the metric conversion. "Ralph Boston came over and said, 'Bob, I think it's over 29'.' I said to Ralph, 'What happened to 28'?'"Beamon recalled.

Boston's math was pretty good: 29'2". Beamon had beaten the world record by 2'. When he realized the magnitude of his accomplishment, he was so thoroughly overcome with emotion that he collapsed and had what doctors later called cataleptic seizure.

Some observers attempted to discredit Beamon's jump, citing Mexico City's thin atmosphere and the just-legal tailwind. But the other jumpers that day came nowhere near the old record, much less Beamon's new one, and in the years that followed, no other jumpers competing at altitude ever approached Beamon's remarkable effort.

Beamon's astonishing world record would last for almost a quarter of a century, until Mike Powell broke it at the 1991 World Championships by only 2". And unlike Beamon, Powell was pushed to the limit. His rival, Carl Lewis, who set the world record in the 100-yard dash only days earlier, broke 29' for the first time in that meet, with a wind-aided jump of 29'2" and a leap of 29'1" against the wind. Powell's record itself has been quite durable, staying on the books for more than 14 years.

Despite that, it is Beamon's effort that is still considered one of the greatest Olympic moments and one of the great individual achievements in sports history, introducing the phrase "Beamonesque" into the lexicon. The man Beamon beat that day, former world record holder Igor Ter-Ovanesyan of the Soviet Union, said it best: "Compared to this jump, we are as children."

JESSE'S JUMP

It was Jesse Owens, not Bob Beamon, who held the long-jump record the longest. Owens set the record of 26'8 $1/4$" on May 25, 1935, as part of a flurry of records during the 1935 Big Ten meet. The mark stood for more than 25 years, until it was broken on August 12, 1960, by future Olympic gold medalist Ralph Boston, who surpassed Owens's record by 3".

BEST AVAILABLE ATHLETE

In the 15th round of the 1969 NBA draft, the Phoenix Suns drafted Bob Beamon. This was the ultimate reach pick, because Beamon had only played basketball as a youngster. Beamon never played in the NBA. But this didn't stop teams from making these kind of stunt picks. The Kansas City Kings drafted decathlon champ Bruce Jenner in 1977 with a seventh-round pick and, in 1984, the Bulls tabbed Carl Lewis on the 10th round.

Critics tried to discredit Beamon's achievement, citing Mexico City's high altitute and a sizeable tailwind, but none of the other competitors came close to the previous record, much less Beamon's incredible distance.

"BOB, I THINK IT'S OVER 29'."
—U.S. OLYMPIC TEAMMATE RALPH BOSTON

"WHAT HAPPENED TO 28'?"
—BOB BEAMON

#10

UNDEFEATED

THE 1972 MIAMI DOLPHINS PROVED THAT PERFECTION IS POSSIBLE IN PRO SPORTS

PERFECTION. IS THERE A MORE ELUSIVE goal in the world of sport or, for that matter, outside it?

That's exactly what the Miami Dolphins achieved during the 1972 season. They went 14–0 in the regular season, and they won three more playoff games. And while undefeated seasons happen with some regularity in college sports, the Dolphins' unblemished campaign is a singular achievement in modern professional sports.

And yet, that Dolphins team is spoken of with respect, but not reverence. When the discussion turns to the greatest football teams of all times, other squads—Pittsburgh's Steel Curtain dynasty, the Vince Lombardi Packers, and the 49ers of the mid-1980s—are usually mentioned before Miami. Why? Perhaps because while their season was perfect, the Dolphins themselves were far from it. "If you were to analyze that roster, our secondary was too slow, our middle linebacker too small, and virtually our entire offensive line had been found off the scrap heap," head coach Don Shula once wrote. "Put me on that list of imperfect parts, too. I couldn't win the big one."

Fresh off a 2–3 loss to the Cowboys in Super Bowl VI, the season hardly started out perfectly for Miami. They went 3–3 in the preseason. In their third game, they found themselves trailing the Minnesota Vikings 14–6 with only 4 1/2 minutes left in the game. Garo Yepremian hit a club-record 51-yard field goal. The comeback was capped by a three-yard TD pass from Bob Griese to Jim Mandich.

Says Griese, "I remember thinking afterward, 'Hey, we must be pretty good.'" Two weeks later, the Dolphins suffered a far bigger scare—Griese broke his leg against the Chargers and was replaced for the rest of the regular season by 38-year-old journeyman Earl Morrall. The next week they survived another close call, edging the Bills 24–23 with Yepremian hitting a 54-yard field goal. But running backs Mercury Morris and Larry Csonka soon picked up the load, becoming the first teammates to rush for more than 1,000 yards each, and the so-called No-Name Defense, led by Nick Buoniconti and Jake Scott, dominated opponents, allowing only 12.2 points per game. The rest of the season was relatively free of drama, and the Dolphins became the first team in 30 years to complete the regular season undefeated.

Entering the playoffs, the Dolphins tried to avoid the fate of the Chicago Bears. In both 1934 and 1942, the Bears were undefeated and untied in the regular season, but were upset in the championship game. In the opening-round playoff game, the Dolphins trailed the Browns in the fourth quarter before Jim Kiick's 8-yard run sealed a 20–14 win. With Griese again seeing action, Miami also trailed the Steelers in the AFC championship game before coming away with a 21–17 victory.

Lloyd Mumphord (left) and Jake Scott (13), part of Miami's "No-Name Defense," break up a pass intended for Washington's Charley Taylor during Super Bowl VII, won 14–7 by the Dolphins.

Despite their unblemished mark, Miami actually entered the Super Bowl as a slight underdog to George Allen's spunky Washington Redskins. In the championship game, the Dolphins were largely in control, but hardly dominant. The most memorable play of the game? The Redskins blocked Garo Yepremian's field goal attempt, and the kicker picked up the ball and tried to pass it to a teammate, but it was instead picked off by Mike Bass for Washington's only touchdown in a 14–7 win. President Richard Nixon commented, "The people of Washington and Miami can both be proud of their teams because they played well."

THE MOST PERFECT

Undefeated seasons are not a rarity in college football. The consensus pick for the most dominant team in modern college football history is the 1995 Nebraska Cornhuskers, which topped "greatest ever" lists compiled by CBS, ESPN, and *Sports Illustrated*. Tom Osborne's charges averaged 53.1 points while running up a 12–0 record, capped by a 62–24 win over second-ranked Florida in the Fiesta Bowl.

HERE'S TO THE LOSERS

It's become a full-fledged urban legend that at the beginning of every NFL season, the surviving members of the 1972 Dolphins each buy a bottle of 1972 champagne. And as the clock runs out on the first defeat for the season's last undefeated team, they pop their corks simultaneously, their perfect record safe for another year.

But it's not true. While the Dolphins have been notably proud of their accomplishment, sometimes to the point of seeming to root against teams that would challenge the record, rumors of an organized Fellowship of the Super Bowl Ring turn out to be nothing more than an urban myth.

"The champagne story is Griese, Dick Anderson, and Nick Buoniconti," says Coach Shula. "They all lived close to each other in Coral Gables, and the one time they did go out and toast each other they were too cheap to invite the rest of us down to the party."

Head coach Don Shula's (center) biggest scare of the perfect season came on October 15, when quarterback Bob Griese was lost for the year with a broken leg.

In the ensuing decades, the Dolphins' record has been challenged, but not seriously. The 1998 Denver Broncos and the 2005 Indianapolis Colts both went 13–0 before losing their next two games. The Dolphins' perfect season was part of a record-tying 18-game winning streak, which was eclipsed by the New England Patriots' 21-game skein in 2003 and 2004.

Football purists will note that the 1948 Cleveland Browns finished 15–0 and won the championship of the old All-America Football Conference. While the Browns later joined the NFL when the AAFC folded, the NFL does not recognize that mark. Cynics will also note that the Dolphins faced a historically weak schedule. They were the only Super Bowl winners since the NFL-AFL merger not to have to face a single playoff team, and their opponents' composite record was a far-less-than-stellar 51–86–3.

But in the end, the Dolphins' mark has stood the test of time, and their distinction as the NFL's first unbeaten team will endure. As Csonka said, "Perfection ends a lot of arguments."

"IF YOU WERE TO ANALYZE THAT ROSTER, OUR SECONDARY WAS TOO SLOW, OUR MIDDLE LINEBACKER TOO SMALL, AND VIRTUALLY OUR ENTIRE OFFENSIVE LINE HAD BEEN FOUND OFF THE SCRAP HEAP. PUT ME ON THAT LIST OF IMPERFECT PARTS, TOO. I COULDN'T WIN THE BIG ONE."
—DON SHULA

11

NOTHING PLUS NOTHING

JOHNNY VANDER MEER'S RECORD OF BACK-TO-BACK NO-HITTERS WILL LIKELY NEVER BE EQUALED, MUCH LESS BROKEN

WANT TO WIN A BAR BET? TURN THE conversation to the subject of sports records that will never be broken. Let your friends cite the usual suspects. The DiMaggio hitting streak. Cy Young's 511 wins. Chamberlain's 100-point game. Then it's your turn.

Johnny Vander Meer's back-to-back no-hitters. It's a feat that's been done exactly once in baseball history, despite the fact that every pitcher goes out and tries to break it every day. (That quest, of course, is usually over by the third inning of the first game, and sometimes by the third batter.)

To break the record, a pitcher would have to throw three consecutive no-hitters. You can collect your winnings now.

The amazing thing of course, is that it wasn't Sandy Koufax or Nolan Ryan who caught lightning in a bottle on two consecutive starts. It was Johnny Vander Meer. Vander Meer wasn't a bad pitcher, but he wasn't a great one either. He was selected for four All-Star games and led the National League in strikeouts three times in a row, from 1941 to 1943. On the other hand, his career record was 119–121 for a winning percentage of .496.

On June 11, 1938, the 22-year-old Vander Meer, who two years prior had been named minor league Player of the Year, earned a start for the Cincinnati Reds against the Boston Bees (a team later to be

"I MISSED THE PITCH"

In a rare display, umpire Bill Stewart admitted to Vander Meer after the game that he made a bad call in the ninth inning of the second no-hitter. Stewart said: "If Leo [Durocher] got a hit, I was to blame, as I missed the pitch and the batter should have been struck out on the previous pitch."

Cincinnati Reds left-hander Johnny Vander Meer warms up after his historic feat of tossing two consecutive no-hitters in June 1938.

Vander Meer in action during the second of his two no-hitters in 1938, against the Brooklyn Dodgers in the first night game played at Ebbets Field.

renamed the Braves.) He announced his presence with authority, retiring the first nine batters he faced. In the top of the fourth, the hard-throwing lefty walked Gene Moore. The next batter, Johnny Cooney, fouled out and Moore strayed off the base and was thrown out when he slipped heading back to first. In the fifth, Vander Meer walked Tony Cuccinello, who was also picked off first.

Although he was known as a hard thrower, on that day Vander Meer struck out only four while walking three in front of a crowd of 10,311 at Crosley Field.

Vander Meer's next start was destined to make history—before he ever took the mound. The June 15 game between the Reds and the Dodgers in Brooklyn marked the first night game in the history of Ebbets Field. There were more than 38,000 in attendance for the festivities and Vander Meer was just an added attraction. No pitcher had ever thrown two no-hitters in a season, and at that point only two had ever managed the feat twice in a career.

Vander Meer had his good stuff, but he flirted with disaster more than he had in his previous start. But in the seventh, when the young lefty walked two batters, the Brooklyn crowd—which included Vander Meer's mother and father and a large contingent from his hometown of Prospect Park, New Jersey—sensing that they might be seeing something special, cheered for him to get out of the jam.

The Reds carried a 6–0 lead into the ninth inning. Vander Meer got Buddy Hassett to ground out for the first out of the inning. Then, perhaps feeling the pressure, Vander Meer walked the bases loaded, prompting a visit from manager Bill McKechnie. "Take it easy, Johnny," he told him. "But get the no-hitter." The next batter, Ernie Koy, hit a grounder to Lou Riggs, who bypassed the double-play chance and instead threw home for the force-out.

With the bases loaded, two outs, and history in the balance, Brooklyn's player/manager Leo Durocher came to the plate. After adding to the drama with

a long foul ball, Vander Meer painted the outside corner, but umpire Bill Stewart, who later admitted he blew the call, called it ball one. Durocher popped up to center field on a 1–2 pitch, and Harry Craft made the historic catch.

The feat made national news, and even president Franklin Delano Roosevelt sent his congratulations. In his next outing, Vander Meer would extend his record of hitless innings to 21²/₃ before giving up a fourth-inning single to Boston's Debs Garms. Vander Meer would never come close to matching this accomplishment, but he would earn yet another place in the record book. On September 11, 1946, the Reds and the Dodgers played a record 19-inning scoreless game at Ebbets Field, the site of Vander Meer's historic game. The Cincinnati lefty pitched the first 15 innings for the Reds, striking out 14.

ALMOST PERFECT

The record for perfect innings belongs to baseball's all-time hard-luck pitcher, Harvey Haddix (above). On May 26, 1959, the Pittsburgh hurler retired the Milwaukee Braves in order in the first inning. And then he did it again. And again and again. Through nine innings, Pittsburgh sent 27 men to the plate, and Haddix sent all 27 right back to the dugout. The only problem: opposing pitcher Lew Burdette, who had scattered nine hits, also had a shutout going, and the pair would take the scoreless duel into extra innings. Haddix retired the Pirates in order three more times, which ran his string of consecutive outs to 36, and broke Waite Hoyt's 1919 record of 34 consecutive batters retired in an extra-inning game. Burdette, however, matched him goose egg for goose egg through 12 innings and retired the Pirates in the top of the thirteenth. In Haddix's unlucky thirteenth, the first batter, Felix Mantilla, reached on a throwing error by third-baseman Don Hoak, which ended the perfect game. Eddie Mathews sacrificed Mantilla to second and Henry Aaron was walked intentionally. The fourth man up in the thirteenth, Joe Adcock, crushed a 1–0 hanging slider just over the wire fence in deep right-center field, which not only ended Haddix's no-hitter and his shutout, but tagged him with the loss as well.

12 61* AND BEYOND

MARIS, McGWIRE, AND BONDS EACH TOOK THEIR OWN SWINGS AT THE BABE'S SINGLE-SEASON HOME-RUN MARK

Babe Ruth watches one of his home runs during his 60-homer season of 1927.

WHILE THE SINGLE-SEASON HOME-RUN record has bounced around some at the turn of the millennium—from the Mark McGwire–Sammy Sosa duel of 1998 to Barry Bonds upping the ante with 73 homers in 2001—the most compelling record attempt came in 1961, when it was a case of the right record and the wrong guy.

When Babe Ruth broke his own home-run record in 1927, there was little sense that he had established an unbreakable standard. Ruth had eclipsed the mark in three consecutive seasons between 1919 and 1921, more than doubling the record from 27 to 59. The expectation was that Ruth, or some other slugger such as teammate Lou Gehrig, would break it again, possibly as soon as the next season.

But as the years went by and Ruth's mark stood unchallenged, with Hall of Famers like Hank Greenberg and Jimmie Foxx mounting an assault but falling well short, the record took on a certain mythic quality. So it hardly seemed likely that a 26-year-old outfielder who had never hit more than 39 home runs (and never would again) would be the man to capture baseball's most storied record.

It certainly wasn't easy for Roger Maris in 1961. The first thing Maris had to overcome was the aura of his New York Yankees teammate Mickey Mantle, who stayed within a few home runs of Maris into mid-

September. If the Babe's record had to be broken, most fans hoped that the popular, telegenic Mantle would be the one to do it, not the plainspoken Maris. A few felt so strongly that they made threats on Maris's life.

Then Baseball Commissioner Ford Frick, who had visited Ruth on his deathbed, got involved. At the suggestion of sportswriter Dick Young, Frick declared that if Maris took more than 154 games of the new 162-game schedule to set the record, it would

THE $3 MILLION BASEBALL

Maris's home-run ball was caught by 19-year-old Sal Durante, who sold the ball to restaurateur Sam Gordon for $5,000. (Gordon ultimately gave the ball, which is now on display at Cooperstown, back to Maris.) By contrast, comic book writer Todd McFarlane, creator of the Spawn series, paid $3 million for Mark McGwire's 70th home-run ball of the 1998 season in 1999 and more than $500,000 for Barry Bonds's 73rd home-run ball of the 2001 season. McFarlane owns nine other home-run balls, including ones hit by McGwire and Sammy Sosa during the 1998 home-run race.

New York Yankees slugger Roger Maris watches the flight of his record-breaking 61ˢᵗ home run of the 1961 season on October 1 at Yankee Stadium.

be marked with an asterisk. The only problem, of course, is that there wasn't any record book and there wasn't any asterisk. Major League Baseball didn't have an official record book at that point, and most of the publishers of independent record books, such as *The Sporting News,* ignored Frick's request.

But the symbolic taint remained. Throughout the summer, benefiting perhaps from facing pitching diluted by expansion, Maris stayed well ahead of Ruth's pace, by as many as 19 games at one point, but as the season drew to a close and the press scrutiny and the pressure increased, he became a basket case, with his hair literally falling out from the stress. The 154ᵗʰ game came and went and Maris had only 59 round-trippers. It wasn't until the 158ᵗʰ game that Maris tied the record and then asked manager Ralph Houk for the day off.

On October 1, 1961, the final game of the season, before a crowd of only 23,154, Maris crushed a 2–0 pitch from Boston's Tracy Stallard to break Ruth's 34-year-old record. Despite the differences in the schedules, it took Maris 698 plate appearances to break the record, while Ruth went to the plate 691 times. One of the strangest pieces of trivia about Maris's record

is that, with the switch-hitting Mantle batting behind him, he didn't draw a single intentional walk in 1961.

Maris, for his part, remained bitter about his treatment that summer.

"They acted as though I was doing something wrong, poisoning the record books or something," he said years later. "Do you know what I have to show for 61 home runs? Nothing. Exactly nothing." Maris died of cancer in 1985 at age 51, his record still intact but also largely unrecognized.

Time has silenced Maris's critics. Although Maris's record hasn't taken on the mythic glow of Ruth's, from a practical point of view it has proved more durable. Maris's record was older than Ruth's when it was broken in 1998 and it took yet another expansion year to make it happen. The home-run race of 1998, when Mark McGwire and Sammy Sosa both broke the old record and swapped the home run lead in the final days of the season, also served to highlight Maris's achievement.

When McGwire hit his 62ⁿᵈ home run, he ran over to the stands to hug the members of the Maris family, and after the game said, "Roger, I hope you're with me tonight." Barry Bonds broke McGwire's record only

> **"Do you know what I have to show for 61 home runs? Nothing. Exactly nothing."**
> —Roger Maris

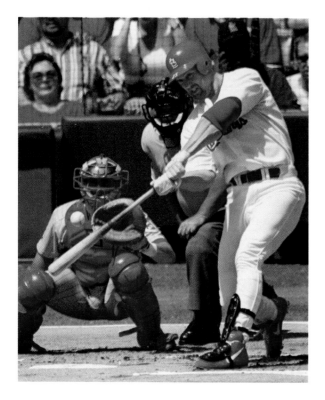 

Mark McGwire (left) launches his 60th homer of the 1998 season en route to a then-record 70 for the year. That record held until Barry Bonds (right) hit his 73rd on October 7, 2001, to rewrite the record books once again.

three years later, despite playing in pitcher-friendly Pac Bell Park. Bonds also broke Babe Ruth's single-season slugging percentage record (.849 set in 1920) with a .863 mark. Bonds also drew 177 walks, breaking Ruth's 1923 record of 170, although Bonds would shatter his own mark with a mind-boggling 232 walks in 2004. "Barry is the reincarnation of Ted Williams—with more power," said his future manager, Felipe Alou.

"You can't tell me the Babe was any better than this guy," said Florida Marlins manager Jack McKeon.

"You can't tell me this guy isn't the best player in the history of the game."

In the wake of the BALCO scandal, the records set by McGwire and Bonds have come into question, although there has been no hard evidence that either used illegal performance-enhancing drugs during their record-setting years. That didn't stop the North Dakota State Legislature from passing a resolution recognizing Maris's mark as the single-season home-run record.

THE OTHER JOLTIN' JOE

Ever heard of Joe Bauman? Until Bonds came along in 2001, Bauman was professional baseball's single-season home-run king. In 1954, playing for the Roswell Rockets in the Class C Longhorn League, he hit a record 72 round-trippers while slugging .916 in only 138 games. He topped the old minor league record of 69, set by Joe Hauser of Minneapolis in 1938 and tied by Bob Crues of Amarillo in 1948. "Number 70 was getting the piano stool off my back. Number 69 was the piano," he said of his record chase, which attracted national attention at the time.

However, the slugging first baseman received no bonus for the record—except for a tip of around $300 from appreciative fans who stuck dollar bills in the chain-link screen behind home plate. Bauman never played a Major League game, and, in fact, never got above Single A ball.

#13

THOROUGHLY UNBEATABLE

AT THE BELMONT, SECRETARIAT SET A
RECORD THAT MAY NEVER BE BROKEN

Secretariat carries jockey Ron Turcotte across the finish line ahead of the field in the 99th Kentucky Derby on May 5, 1973.

HORSES DON'T READ THE RECORD BOOK. While records in sports contested by humans are, as they say, made to be broken, and are always on the minds of the top competitors, horses, even the best Thoroughbreds, have no such ambition.

Which is why the records set by Secretariat are so amazing. In the 1973 Kentucky Derby, the chestnut stallion began the Triple Crown quest in style. He became the first horse to break the two-minute mark, with a time of 1:59.40. What was even more unusual is that Secretariat actually seemed to gain speed throughout the race, running each quarter mile faster than the previous one, and the final leg in a blistering 23 seconds flat. This is all but unheard of in the world of racing, where even horses with so-called late speed slow down late in the race, albeit somewhat less than their tiring competitors.

Secretariat was an amazing physical specimen, but the real secret was hidden deep inside. When he was necropsied after his death, the size of his heart was found to be more than 20 pounds, roughly three times the size of an average Thoroughbred's.

In the Preakness, Secretariat did not falter, but the timekeeper did. Jockey Ron Turcotte took Secretariat to an early lead with a bold early move and comfortably held off second-place finisher Sham by two lengths. The electronic timer yielded a time of 1:55, which was clearly too slow. The track's clocker came up with a time of 1:54^2/$_5$. But two veteran clockers from the *Daily Racing Form*, working from independent vantage points, each timed the race a full second faster at 1:53^2/$_5$.

The controversy continued after the race, and CBS Sports ran a side-by-side synchronized replay of Secretariat's Preakness and Canonero II's 1971 track-record race. Although Secretariat crossed the line first in the video showdown, the Maryland Jockey Club took the middle ground and went with the 1:54^2/$_5$ timing. The *Daily Racing Form* registered its dissent by listing both times in its summary of the race.

Then came the Belmont Stakes. Before the race, the focus was on the Triple Crown, a feat which had not been achieved since Citation did it in 1948. It was this buzz that landed Secretariat on the cover of *Time, Newsweek,* and *Sports Illustrated.* But the will-he-or-won't-he drama was over pretty quickly. As his only serious rival, Sham, tired, Secretariat's lead grew from seven lengths to 20 to an astonishing 31 lengths over

Twice a Prince as he crossed the line. The margin was so huge that officials had to consult photos to determine the actual distance.

Even more spectacular was the time of 2:24, which was not only a Belmont Stakes record but which also represented the fastest mile-and-a-half ever run in the U.S. He broke the 16-year-old track record by 2^3/$_5$ seconds, the equivalent of 16 lengths. In the more than three decades since, no horse has come within two seconds of the mark. The amazing thing is that Secretariat was never challenged in the race, and jockey Ron Turcotte suggested that the horse could have run even faster.

"I know this sounds crazy, but the horse did it by himself. I was along for the ride."

Perhaps. Charles Hatton of the *Daily Racing Form* summed up that amazing Belmont record best: "His only point of reference is himself."

> ## "I KNOW THIS SOUNDS CRAZY, BUT THE HORSE DID IT BY HIMSELF. I WAS ALONG FOR THE RIDE."
> —SECRETARIAT'S JOCKEY RON TURCOTTE

Secretariat and Turcotte (front left) completed the historic Triple Crown with a dominating 31-length victory at the Belmont Stakes on June 9, 1973.

WANNA WIN A BAR BET?

Who ran the second-fastest Kentucky Derby? It's the answer to a classic bar bet. After Secretariat's run, the obvious answer was Northern Dancer, who set the previous record of 2:00.00 flat in 1964. In 2001, Monarchos became the second-fastest winner with a time of 1:59.97. But even knowledgeable racing fans often forget about another contender. Sham finished one and a half lengths behind Secretariat in 1973. Using the formula that one length is equal to two-tenths of a second, Sham's time works out to 1:59.90.

14

THE KING OF SWING

TY COBB'S CAREER BATTING AVERAGE OF .366 HAS NEVER BEEN BETTERED

Known as the "Georgia Peach," Cobb played in the majors for 24 seasons, beginning at the age of 18 in 1905.

IN TODAY'S BASEBALL, BATTING .366 FOR a season is likely to earn a player not only a batting title, but an eight-figure contract extension as well. That's what Ty Cobb averaged over a 24-year career.

The Tigers' center fielder owned a variety of records when he retired—career hits, career steals, runs scored—and one by one they fell by the wayside. But his career batting average endures and has become his legacy.

"Every great batter works on the theory that the pitcher is more afraid of him than he is of the pitcher," Cobb said of his craft. And pitchers had plenty of reasons to be afraid of Cobb. There's a reasonable argument to be made for Cobb's being the greatest hitter of all time.

While hitting .400 has been an impossible dream for more than 60 years, Cobb did it three times. And while he played in the dead-ball era, he was one of the liveliest hitters of his day, leading the AL in slugging percentage seven times in eight years. He led the league in on-base percentage seven times, and he even won one home run crown (albeit with only nine round-trippers back in 1909).

But what defined Cobb was his batting average. He won his first batting title in 1907, hitting .350, which began one of the most amazing streaks in baseball history—Cobb's run of nine batting titles in a row.

That streak ended in 1916 when Cobb hit a mere .371 and was beaten for the batting title by Tris Speaker. The Georgia Peach came back the next year and ran his skein to 12 of 13. In 1922, he hit .401, but he was beaten out for the batting title by George Sisler, who hit .420.

While Cobb was respected and feared, he was not well liked. In 1909, for example, he sharpened his spikes and cut A's third baseman Frank Baker. The incident stirred up so much bad blood that Cobb received death threats and needed a police escort in Philadelphia. One incident from 1910 sums up the Georgia Peach's relationship with his rivals. Cobb entered the final day of the season with a comfortable lead over Napoleon Lajoie in the batting race. But Cobb was so hated that the Browns, who were playing Lajoie's Cleveland Naps, attempted to throw the batting race.

"EVERY GREAT BATTER WORKS ON THE THEORY THAT THE PITCHER IS MORE AFRAID OF HIM THAN HE IS OF THE PITCHER."
—TY COBB

His aggressive style on the base paths probably didn't earn Cobb too many extra points on his career batting average, but it certainly helped to build his legacy as one of the game's all-time greats.

COBB CORRECTED

As the game's first truly great player, Cobb was affected more than any other by the recent attempts to clean up the game's statistical records. For example, a game-by-game analysis of the 1910 batting race revealed that an accounting error earlier in the year had double-counted two Cobb hits. If not for the mistake, Lajoie would have won the title by a point. Similar accounting issues, which increased the number of Cobb's career at-bats slightly, also took a point from Cobb's career batting average, which is why it sits at .366 in most of today's record books instead of the .367 figure that was cited for more than half a century.

Ty Cobb, shown here during the 1928 season, won an amazing nine batting titles in a row.

An outfielder "misplayed" a Lajoie fly ball into a triple in the first inning. Then the Browns' manager, Jack O'Connor, instructed his third baseman, Red Corriden, to play deep, all the way on the edge of the outfield grass, allowing Lajoie to collect bunt hit after bunt hit. Nap went eight for nine on the afternoon. Despite that, Cobb still ended up winning the batting title by the narrowest of margins, .384944 to .384084. (The upshot: the Chalmers Motor Car Company, which was sponsoring a batting-race giveaway, awarded a vehicle to both Cobb and Lajoie. O'Connor was run out of baseball by American League president Ban Johnson.)

That's the Cobb story in a nutshell: he was so good that even an out-and-out conspiracy couldn't keep him down. He won a record 12 batting crowns, well ahead of Tony Gwynn and Honus Wagner with eight each. His .366 batting average is eight points better than that of Rogers Hornsby, who's second on the list, and a whopping 28 points better than Gwynn's, the best hitter of baseball's post-expansion era.

Said Joe DiMaggio, "Every time I hear of this guy again, I wonder how he was possible."

#15 URSA MAJORS

COMBINE THE CAREERS OF ANY TWO GOLF LEGENDS, AND JACK NICKLAUS PROBABLY WON MORE MAJOR TITLES

Of his 18 major tournament victories, Jack Nicklaus probably shone brightest in his last, the 1986 Masters at age 45.

HOW MUCH RESONANCE DOES JACK Nicklaus's record of 18 major championships have? A nine-year-old Tiger Woods tacked the list up on his bedroom wall, knowing that if he wanted to be known as the world's greatest golfer, that was the benchmark.

In the days before Tiger, Nicklaus was the game's prodigy. He won the first of his six Ohio State junior titles at the age of 12. At age 18, Nicklaus attended Ohio State University, where he captured two U.S. Amateur titles, in 1959 and 1961, and won the NCAA championship in 1961. In 1960, as an amateur, he finished second to Arnold Palmer at the U.S. Open. Turning pro in 1962, Nicklaus captured his first major, winning the U.S. Open at age 22. He defeated Palmer, who was then the game's best and most popular player, in an 18-hole playoff.

"Now that the big guy's out of the cage, everybody ought to run for cover," said Palmer of the golfer who was then known simply as Fat Jack.

Using a combination of power from the tees and precision putting, Nicklaus began a remarkable run that would see him win 17 more majors over the next 24 years. "He played a game with which I am not familiar," said the great Bobby Jones. By age 26, Nicklaus had won the career Grand Slam—a feat accomplished by only four other golfers—and by the end of his career had won each major at least three

Nicklaus and caddy Willie Peterson celebrate a birdie putt on 16 in the opening round of the 1972 Masters. The Golden Bear would claim that tournament as one of his six overall Masters championships.

times. (Woods is the only other golfer to win each major twice.) He would collect a total of 18 majors: six Masters, five PGA Championships, four U.S. Opens, and three British Opens. To put that win total in perspective, Nicklaus not only buried Walter Hagen's previous record of 11, he collected more majors than Ben Hogan (nine), considered by many to be the greatest golfer ever, and Bobby Jones (seven) combined. His approach was simple.

"I never went into a tournament or round of golf thinking I had to beat a certain player. I had to beat the golf course. If I prepared myself for a major, went in focused, and then beat the golf course, the rest took care of itself."

Nicklaus's hallmark was consistency. He played in 154 consecutive majors for which he was eligible and finished in the top ten 73 times—nearly 50 percent. Over a 15-year run in the British Open between 1966 and 1980, Nicklaus never finished worse than sixth.

Nicklaus capped off his remarkable run of majors in style, with his most memorable victory—the 1986 Masters. Entering the tournament, Nicklaus hadn't won a major in nearly six years, and columnist Tom

McCollister of *The Atlanta Journal-Constitution* merely said what many were thinking when he suggested that it might be time for Nicklaus to retire. Nicklaus's longtime friend John Montgomery posted the column on the refrigerator of the condo they were sharing that week.

Nicklaus started the back nine that day five shots behind the leader and had to battle against legends like Seve Ballesteros, Tom Kite, and Greg Norman, who were all in the prime of their careers. The CBS broadcast crew had been instructed to ignore Nicklaus and focus on the leaders.

Before the start of the final round, Nicklaus's son Steve called him and said, "Pop, what's it going to take?"

"A 65," Jack replied.

"Well, go ahead and do it," challenged his son.

ALMOST LIKE ROYALTY

Although he only won the British Open three times, Jack Nicklaus's performance in the tournament is remarkable. He finished as a runner-up seven times, and from 1966 to 1980, he never finished worse than sixth. This performance led to a singular honor; in 2005 Nicklaus became the first living nonroyal person to appear on a bank note in the United Kingdom. The Royal Bank of Scotland issued a five-pound note to commemorate Nicklaus's last appearance at the British Open at St. Andrews.

With his oldest son, Jack Jr., caddying for him, Nicklaus caught fire. He birdied the 11th, the first hole of Amen Corner, but gave the shot back with a bogey on 12, which Nicklaus considered the turning point of the historic round.

"I don't know why, but it really got me going," he said. "I knew I couldn't play defensively with the rest of the course. I knew I needed to be aggressive."

The Golden Bear birdied the par-5 13th hole. On the par-5 15th, he hit his 4 iron to within 12 feet of the hole and sank the putt for eagle. Nicklaus continued to ravage Augusta National, birdying the par-3 16th and Par-4 17th to take the lead. He sealed this remarkable round with a par to complete an amazing back-nine 30 and a 65 for the round. Donning the green jacket over the red sweater capped not only a great round and a great tournament, but perhaps the greatest career.

That said, Nicklaus's record for majors is in real, if not imminent danger. By his 30th birthday in 2005, Tiger Woods had already won 10 majors. That puts Woods in an interesting position. He's ahead of Nicklaus's pace, but he still trails by eight titles, more than Arnold Palmer was able to manage in a career. But whether he breaks the record or falls short, Tiger's pursuit will only serve to highlight the accomplishments of the game's greatest golfer—and its greatest record.

Nicklaus clutches the PGA National Championship trophy at Cleveland's Canterbury Golf Club in 1973. This was one of five PGA championships he won during his career.

FIRST IN SECONDS

What would you call a player who finished second in a major championship more often than he won them? Jack Nicklaus. The Golden Bear finished second in a major an astonishing 19 times, including seven second-place finishes at the British Open. Some of his opponents attributed this to the fact that he was overextended without side business interests. "He's a legend in his spare time," said Chi Chi Rodriguez. Whatever the reason, Nicklaus often found himself on the short end of some of golf's greatest moments. In the 1982 U.S. Open at Pebble Beach, he watched as Tom Watson chipped in from the heavy rough to set up his miracle victory.

"IF I PREPARED MYSELF FOR A MAJOR, WENT IN FOCUSED, AND THEN BEAT THE GOLF COURSE, THE REST TOOK CARE OF ITSELF."
—JACK NICKLAUS

#16

MUST-SEE TD

JOHNNY UNITAS'S 47-GAME TD STREAK IS
ONE OF THE NFL'S MOST ENDURING MARKS

IN THE HIT-AND-BE-HIT WORLD OF THE NFL, suiting up every Sunday for almost five years is a noteworthy accomplishment. Between 1956 and 1960, Johnny Unitas of the Baltimore Colts did that and far more. He threw a touchdown in 47 consecutive games. During the streak, Unitas completed 697 passes for 10,645 yards. What's more impressive, he threw 102 touchdown passes, averaging more than two scores a game.

Unitas started his streak on December 9, 1956, against the Rams. It began modestly enough with a three-yard TD pass to end Jim Mutscheller in a 31–7 loss to L.A. at the L.A. Coliseum.

Forty-six games later, on December 4, 1960, in a 20–15 loss to the Detroit Lions, Unitas threw two TD passes to Lenny Moore, 80 and 38 yards. The next week, on December 11, Unitas was kept off the scoreboard in a 10–3 loss to the Rams in Los Angeles.

Colts receiver Raymond Berry pulls in a 13-yard touchdown pass from Johnny Unitas on September 25, 1960, running Unitas's streak of consecutive games with a TD pass to 38.

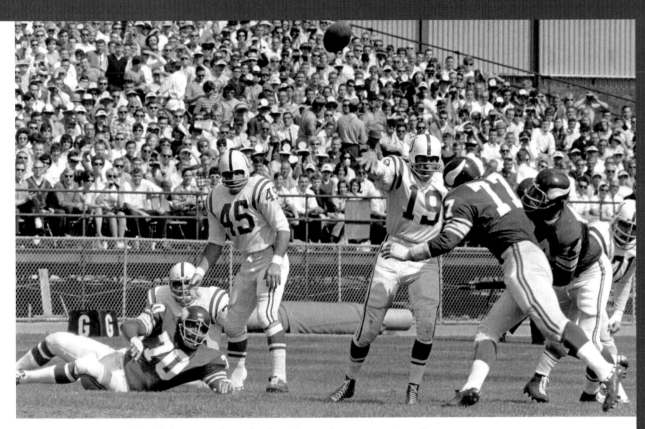

Six years after the streak ended, Unitas threw for four TDs in this game against the Vikings to surpass Y. A. Tittle for the most career touchdown passes with 214.

SNAP AFTER SNAP

While Johnny Unitas's touchdown record is certainly an endurance mark of a kind, the real ironman among NFL quarterbacks is Brett Favre of the Green Bay Packers. As of the conclusion of the 2005 NFL season, Favre had played in 205 consecutive regular-season games, and 225 games including playoff contests. Favre's streak began in October of 1992 against the Pittsburgh Steelers, and he has played through a variety of injuries, including a broken thumb on his throwing hand, and personal tragedies, including the death of his father.

Raymond Berry and Moore, both Hall of Famers themselves, were Johnny U's favorite targets with 38 and 27 TD catches during the streak.

"There was no doubt he was going to be there every single day and give you absolutely everything he had," Moore recalled. "But it was not just about effort. He had incredible touch and accuracy. As far as I'm concerned, he was the best and that record will never be broken."

During the streak, Unitas displayed his incredible toughness. He was not very mobile in the pocket and used to absorb some shockingly heavy hits in the days before rule changes designed to protect the passer were implemented. In one game against the Bears, Chicago defensive end Doug Atkins got through All-Pro offensive tackle Jim Parker and busted Unitas across the nose. Blood spurted everywhere and offensive guard Alex Sandusky scooped up some mud and stuffed it up Unitas's nose to stop the bleeding.

"I almost got sick when I looked at that," Parker said. "But he kept on playing and didn't even think of coming out. He was the toughest player I ever saw."

> "THERE WAS NO DOUBT HE WAS GOING TO BE THERE EVERY SINGLE DAY AND GIVE YOU
> ABSOLUTELY EVERYTHING HE HAD. BUT IT WAS NOT JUST ABOUT EFFORT.
> HE HAD INCREDIBLE TOUCH AND ACCURACY. AS FAR AS I'M CONCERNED,
> HE WAS THE BEST AND THAT RECORD WILL NEVER BE BROKEN."
> —LENNY MOORE

On the other hand, Unitas showed that he could give as good as he got. "A guy broke through the line, hit him, pushed his head in the ground," recalls defensive end Bubba Smith, who played with Unitas later in his career. "He called the same play, let the guy come through, and broke his nose with the football. I said, 'That's my hero.'"

Even though the NFL has become more passer-friendly, Unitas's record has yet to be seriously challenged. Second on the list is Brett Favre of the Green Bay Packers, who compiled a 36-game streak between 2002 and 2004. Dan Marino put together a 30-game streak between 1985 and 1987, and Dave Krieg of the Seattle Seahawks threw for a score in 28 consecutive games between 1983 and 1985.

To put Unitas's feat in some perspective, while Peyton Manning managed to put together a 27-game streak, the Colts star has never had one full season in which he threw at least one TD pass in every game, not even his 2004 campaign when he threw a record 49 TDs. Similarly, neither Joe Montana, John Elway, nor Steve Young ever came within a season of Unitas's mark.

While football fans speak of this mark with a reverence usually reserved for Joe DiMaggio's 56-game hitting streak, Unitas, who died in 2002 of a heart attack, always downplayed the record. "That was just something that was part of my job," Unitas said. "I was out there to help us win games. Putting touchdowns on the board helped us win. That's it."

OIL BARON

Johnny Unitas was a ninth-round draft pick in 1955 and was ultimately cut by the Pittsburgh Steelers. Because it was too late to hook up with another NFL team, Unitas played with the semipro Bloomfield Rams, a team that had to sprinkle its barren playing field with oil to keep the dust down. His salary was $3 a game.

#17 A WHIFF OF FAME

NOLAN RYAN'S CAREER STRIKEOUT RECORD IS A PRODUCT OF POWER AND ENDURANCE

Nolan Ryan's career strikeouts record seems all but untouchable. He was arguably the most durable pitcher of all time.

To put a record out of reach, it takes a perfect storm of just the right circumstances, and Nolan Ryan came along at just the right time to set an all-but-unbreakable mark. And that's why Nolan Ryan's all-time career strikeout mark will likely stand for a very, very long time.

The first component of this kind of record run is simple. You've got to have the right guy. And Ryan was that. He threw hard. Real hard. It's easy to undersell Ryan's dominance because he was so far ahead of his time. Over his career he struck out 9.55 men per nine innings. How does that compare to the other great pitchers of all time? Steve Carlton struck out 7.14. Tom Seaver? 6.85. And the great Walter Johnson, who held the strikeout record before Ryan broke it? A mere 5.34.

If you look at the current leaders in Ks per nine innings, all of the contenders are contemporary pitchers except for Sandy Koufax and Sudden Sam McDowell, neither of whom had a long career. So you might say that Ryan was ahead of his time. But at the same time, the times they were a-changing. When Ryan was breaking in, there was a sea change regarding hitters' attitudes about striking out.

Joe DiMaggio's claim to fame was the fact that he hardly ever fanned—only 369 times. (Although trivia buffs will note that his brother Vince held the

JUST ONE HIT

The only player to have his jersey retired by three teams—the Angels, the Rangers, and the Astros—Ryan also pitched a record seven no-hitters, his first on May 15, 1973, against the Royals. His last was on May 1, 1991, against Toronto. Ryan also threw 12 one-hitters during his career, but he shares that record with Hall of Famer Bob Feller.

Ryan tips his cap after ringing up his 10th strikeout for the 97th time in his career back in 1977, tying Sandy Koufax for the record.

OVER HIS CAREER RYAN STRUCK OUT **9.55** MEN PER NINE INNINGS.
HOW DOES THAT COMPARE TO THE OTHER GREAT PITCHERS OF ALL TIME?
STEVE CARLTON STRUCK OUT **7.14**. TOM SEAVER—**6.85**. AND THE
GREAT WALTER JOHNSON, WHO HELD THE STRIKEOUT RECORD BEFORE
RYAN BROKE IT, STRUCK OUT A MERE **5.34**.

single-season strikeout record for 18 years.) Mickey Mantle was a legendary free swinger, and demolished Babe Ruth's career strikeout record. The Mick helped to erase the stigma behind the strikeout, and that, coupled with the pitcher-friendly conditions of the 1960s (a higher mound, larger ballparks), helped to start an overall increase in strikeouts that continues to this day.

If that's the case, why isn't Ryan's record in serious jeopardy from some contemporary fireballer? Because of the other aspect of the perfect storm equation. Ryan broke in at a time when pitchers pitched far more than they do today. Four-man rotations and complete games were very much the norm. In 1974, when Ryan led the American League, he threw $332^2/_3$ innings. By contrast, the 2005 league leader, Mark Buehrle, threw almost 100 fewer innings, $236^2/_3$. Buehrle pitched three complete games. Ryan threw 26 in 1974—and yet he finished fourth in the American League in that category.

Add to that the simple fact that Ryan was one of the most durable pitchers in major league history. He started his career at 19 and ended it at 46, and in between he was always there to take the ball. Between

1971 and 1992, he never threw fewer than 149 innings. That's why Ryan was able to throw 5,386 innings, which ranks him fifth all time, behind three legends from the dead-ball era—Cy Young, Pud Galvin, and Walter Johnson—plus Phil Niekro, a knuckleballer.

Which is why Randy Johnson and Roger Clemens don't have the proverbial snowball's chance of catching Ryan. Clemens's strikeout ratio (8.61 K/9) is lower than Ryan's and at age 42, entering the 2006 season, he's thrown $4,704^1/_3$ innings, which leaves The Rocket $681^2/_3$ behind Ryan.

The Big Unit has a similar problem. His strikeout ratio is the best of all time (10.95 K/9 entering the 2006 season), but at age 42, he's only thrown $3,593^2/_3$ innings. That puts him 1792.3 innings behind Ryan. To put that in perspective, that's just about as many innings as Barry Zito and Mark Prior had combined entering the 2006 season.

Ryan combined modern-day strikeout ratios with old-school inning totals. And with inning totals going down faster than strikeout ratios are going up, none of today's pitchers has a realistic shot of deposing Ryan as baseball's all-time strikeout king.

THE KING OF WALKS

Who holds the record for bases on balls? That too would be Nolan Ryan, and his total of 2,795, well ahead of Steve Carlton's 1,833, looks to be just as unassailable as his strikeout record. And that's Nolan Ryan in a nutshell—an exceptional pitcher, but not necessarily a great one. He's got 324 wins, but he's also got 292 losses, third all time and only 24 behind Cy Young. Ryan's .526 winning percentage is downright ordinary. He never won a Cy Young award and won 20 games only twice. So it's a testament to the power of the strikeout that in Ryan's first year of eligibility for the Hall of Fame, he received a record 491 votes.

#18 RUSHING ROULETTE

WHICH NFL RUNNING BACK SET THE MOST IMPRESSIVE RECORD?

MOST RUSHING YARDS IN AN NFL SEASON. You'd think that a record like that would be a no-brainer for a list like this, and you'd be right. But which version of the record is really most enduring? Let's look at the candidates.

Jim Brown: "Make sure when anyone tackles you he remembers how much it hurts." That was Brown's advice to a young running back, and he never lived those words more fully than in his 1963 season, which was one of the most impressive in football history. The poetically inclined will note that with 1,863 yards, he was the first back in league history to rush for more than a mile in a single season. The statistically minded will note that he broke the record with a modest 291 carries. That averages out to a stunning 6.4 yards per carry. To put it another way, every time that Brown carried the ball, the Cleveland Browns were almost two-thirds of the way to a first down. Brown also broke Joe Perry's career rushing record in the sixth week of the season, and won yet another MVP award.

O. J. Simpson: sure, it's nearly impossible, in the wake of his murder trial, to assess Simpson's football career objectively. But in 1973, the former Heisman Trophy winner not only lived up to the hype, he put together a season for the ages. Simpson started strong and finished stronger, running for 219 yards in the next-to-last game, against New England, and another

200 in the season finale, against the Jets. He not only passed Brown, but he became the first back to rush for 2,000 yards. Several others have achieved that milestone since—Terrell Davis, Jamal Lewis, Barry Sanders, and Eric Dickerson—but all did it in a 16-game season. Which brings us to the most impressive aspect of his season, statistically speaking. Simpson averaged 143 yards per game, which is 10 yards a game more than Brown.

Eric Dickerson: Dickerson is the Roger Maris of NFL running backs. When he broke Simpson's record in 1984, many fans put a sort of unwritten asterisk next to his total of 2,105 yards. The season had been expanded from 14 to 16 games in 1978, and the reasonable expectation was that the record eventually would be broken. Critics also note that Dickerson's 132-yard-per-game total was lower than both Brown's and Simpson's. And yet this mark has proven to be surprisingly durable. It's been challenged—by Davis, Lewis, and Sanders—but it's still on the books. And at 20 years and counting it's been more durable than both Brown's and Simpson's marks, which stood only 10 and 11 years respectively.

So which running back gets the nod? Each of these classic seasons has its merits but the most relevant stat is yards-per-game, which gives a narrow nod to Orenthal James Simpson.

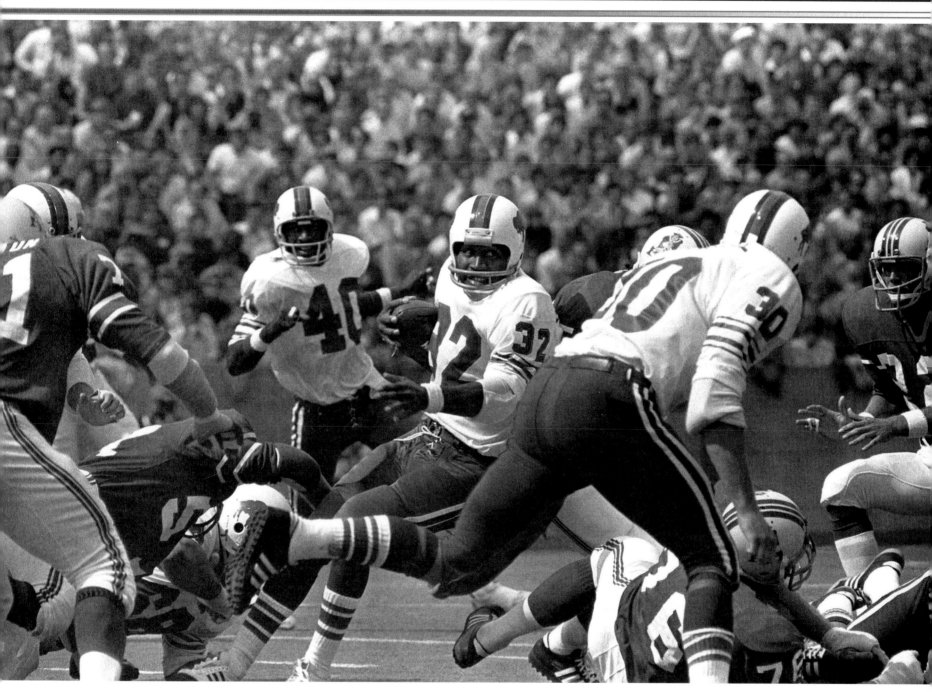

Buffalo's O. J. Simpson finds an opening against the New England Patriots during a September game at the start of his historic 1973 season.

SIMPSON STARTED STRONG AND FINISHED STRONGER, RUNNING FOR **219**
YARDS IN THE NEXT-TO-LAST GAME, AGAINST NEW ENGLAND, AND
ANOTHER **200** IN THE SEASON FINALE, AGAINST THE JETS.

Buffalo's O. J. Simpson breaks a big gain against the New York Jets on December 16, 1973, the day he surpassed the 2,000-yard mark for the season.

RUSHING TO CLASS

Which collegian rushed for the most yards in a season? That would be another NFL star, Barry Sanders. The Oklahoma State star ran for 2,628 yards in 1988. His 238 yards per game is also a Division 1-A record, making him only the third back—Marcus Allen of USC and Ed Marinaro of Cornell are the others—to rush for more than 200 yards per game over the course of a season.

The NCAA record for single game rushing belongs to another NFL superstar, LaDainian Tomlinson. The TCU star rushed for 404 yards against UTEP on November 20, 1999. Tomlinson carried the ball 43 times, topping the 1991 mark of 396 yards on 58 carries set by Tony Sands of Kansas. Tomlinson also scored six touchdowns that afternoon. Tomlinson's mark dwarfs the NFL single-game record of 295, set by Jamal Lewis of Baltimore against Cleveland in 2003.

"All the credit goes to the offensive line," said Tomlinson after his achievement. "They've done a great job of creating holes all season. I need to buy them a couple of steaks." The all-time collegiate record is 441 yards, set by Dante Brown of Division III Marietta College in 1996.

RUNNING ON EMPTY

For all the emphasis on the running game in football, the NFL teams that these three Hall of Fame backs played for enjoyed only modest postseason success. Neither Simpson nor Dickerson won a Super Bowl—or even played in the big game. Paul Brown's Cleveland Browns won an NFL championship in 1964, but the team won three titles in six years just before Brown's arrival.

#19 FOR PETE'S SAKE

NO COLLEGE PLAYER EVER SCORED MORE THAN LSU'S "PISTOL" PETE MARAVICH

Pete Maravich of Louisiana State University goes up for two points late in the 1968–69 season.

CONSIDER THIS: AT THE TIME PETE Maravich scored a record 3,667 points at Louisiana State University, the NCAA had prohibited freshmen from playing varsity basketball. That means that Pistol Pete scored more in three years than anyone's been able to do since with four years in which to try. Chew on that for a moment. Then remember that there were also no three-point field goals.

And finally consider what the record might have been if Maravich had been allowed to play all four years. After all, he averaged 43.6 points on LSU's freshman team. Maravich was simply the greatest scorer in the history of college basketball.

The total-points record is only the tip of the statistical iceberg for Maravich. His 44.2-point career average is also a record, as is his senior year average of 44.5 points. His sophomore (43.8) and junior year (44.2) scoring averages rank second and third of all time. He owns single-season records for field goals made (1,387) and free throws made (893). His 69 points against

Alabama set a single-game record that stood for 21 years. Today, scoring 50 makes news. Maravich scored 50 points or more 28 times in only 84 games—fully one-third of his games—including 10 times in his senior year. He scored 60 or more points four times, three in his senior season. Again, both are records.

The son of LSU coach Press Maravich, Pete honed his skills through obsessive practice, dribbling while riding his bicycle, insisting on an aisle seat in the movie theatre so he could dribble while he watched.

"I'd do incredible things," Maravich recalled. "I would dribble blindfolded in the house. I would take my basketball to bed with me; I'd lay there after my mother kissed and tucked me in, and I'd shoot the ball up in the air and say, 'Fingertip control, backspin, follow-through.'"

At age 12, he told a reporter about his ambitions: "To play pro basketball, get a big diamond ring, and make a million dollars." Maravich went on to do all of those things, but his pro career was similar to his

> "I WOULD DRIBBLE BLINDFOLDED IN THE HOUSE. I WOULD TAKE MY BASKETBALL TO BED WITH ME; I'D LAY THERE AFTER MY MOTHER KISSED AND TUCKED ME IN, AND I'D SHOOT THE BALL UP IN THE AIR AND SAY, 'FINGERTIP CONTROL, BACKSPIN, FOLLOW-THROUGH.'"
> —PETE MARAVICH

FOR 72 POINTS...
AND A LOSS

While most of Maravich's scoring records remain on the books, one important mark has been broken: his all-time single-game scoring record of 69 points, scored in a 106–104 loss to Alabama on February 7, 1970. Kevin Bradshaw of U.S. International broke Maravich's NCAA Division I single-game scoring record with 72 points against Loyola Marymount, on January 5, 1991. As with Maravich, Bradshaw's heroics went in vain: U.S. International lost the game to Loyola 186–140, with Loyola Marymount's scoring total setting an NCAA record. Maravich still holds three of the top nine single-game marks.

Maravich went on to star in the NBA and led the league in scoring in 1977 with a 31.1 points-per-game average.

SHE SHOOTS, SHE SCORES

Lynette Woodward—3,649

The women's game doesn't have its own Pete Maravich. The NCAA Division I career leader is Jackie Stiles of Southwest Missouri State, who finished her collegiate career in 2001 with 3,393 points. And in her senior year she became the first women's collegiate player to score 1,000 points in a season. She broke the career record of 3,122 career points held by Patricia Hoskins who starred at Mississippi Valley State from 1985 to 1989.

However, Stiles is still not the all-time collegiate leader. That honor goes to Lynette Woodward of Kansas, who scored 3,649 points at the University of Kansas from 1977 to 1981 when the AIAW was the sanctioning body for women's college basketball. The NCAA Division I single-game record is the 60 points scored by Cindy Brown of Long Beach State against San Jose State on February 16, 1987. The AIAW mark is 70 points, scored by Annette Kennedy of SUNY-Purchase against Pratt on January 22, 1984.

college career—great personal achievements, but fewer wins and championships than you might expect.

Indeed, Maravich is the poster boy for those fans who argue that statistics are meaningless. Despite Maravich's heroics, LSU never made the NCAA tournament even once during his career. With Pete's father Press as head coach, LSU went 49–35 and their only postseason foray was a third-place finish in the 1970 NIT.

Why didn't his teams do better? The record book holds a clue to something that LSU's opponents realized after a while. Maravich attempted an NCAA-record 3,166 shots in his career. Pistol Pete shot more in three seasons than any recent player has been able to hoist in four.

#20 MAN OF THE HOUR

IN 60 MINUTES ONE AFTERNOON, JESSE OWENS SET FOUR WORLD RECORDS

JAMES CLEVELAND "JESSE" OWENS IS BEST remembered for his heroics in the 1936 Munich Olympics, where he won gold medals and embarrassed host Adolf Hitler. But as impressive as he was during those games, his best afternoon came a year earlier at the 1935 Big Ten Championships, while competing for Ohio State.

Owens started the afternoon by tying his own world record in the 100-yard dash, set when he was a senior in high school, with a time of 9.4 seconds. But that was just a warm-up. Ten minutes later, at the long jump pit, Owens marked off the current world record, dropping a hanky 26'2" from the takeoff. On his first attempt, he jumped 26'8", breaking the old mark by 6" and setting a record that would last for 25 years.

But he was not done. Nine minutes later, he shattered another mark, breaking a world record in the 220-yard dash (and the shorter 200-meter dash as well). And then he took a breather—all of 24 minutes—before he obliterated the world record in the 220-yard hurdles.

Think that's amazing? The week before the meet, Owens had fallen down a flight of stairs. He injured his back so badly that it was questionable whether he would be able to compete at all, and he had been taking treatment right up to the start of the first race. It was only after his coaches saw his record-worthy per-

formance in the 100 that he was allowed to compete in the other events.

A year later Owens would stun the world by winning an unprecedented four track and field gold medals in the 1936 Olympics games—the 100-meter, 200-meter, long jump, and 4 x 100 relay. (This feat would be equaled by Carl Lewis in 1984.) The legend is that Adolf Hitler, embarrassed by the defeat, refused to shake Owens's hand. The reality was a little more complex: early in the Games, Hitler congratulated several German winners and then left the stadium. The International Olympic Committee decreed that he had to acknowledge every champion or none at all, and the German chancellor chose the latter course.

There has been speculation that Owens was actually the beneficiary of the behind-the-scenes politics of the games. Two Jewish athletes, Marty Glickman and Sam Stoller, were pulled off the 4 x 100 relay team at the last moment and replaced by Owens and Ralph Metcalfe. It is thought that this was a concession to the host country, where anti-Semitism ran deeper than racism. And in his autobiography Owens himself suggested that Hitler stood up and waved to him in the stadium.

Unlike today, when Olympic gold medalists can choose from a wide variety of commercial opportunities, Owens found slim pickings back home. "After I

THE WEEK BEFORE THE MEET, OWENS FELL DOWN A FLIGHT OF STAIRS. HE INJURED HIS BACK SO BADLY THAT IT WAS QUESTIONABLE WHETHER OR NOT HE WOULD BE ABLE TO COMPETE AT ALL AND WAS TAKING TREATMENT RIGHT UP TO THE START OF THE FIRST RACE. IT WAS ONLY AFTER HIS COACHES SAW HIS RECORD-WORTHY PERFORMANCE IN THE 100 THAT HE WAS ALLOWED TO COMPETE IN THE OTHER EVENTS.

Jesse Owens of Ohio State hits the finish line well ahead of his Big Ten competitors during a 1935 meet in which he set the world record for the 220-yard dash.

Owens also set a new mark in the long jump, beating the old mark by six inches and setting a new standard that would last 25 years.

came home from the 1936 Olympics with my four medals, it became increasingly apparent that everyone was going to slap me on the back, want to shake my hand, or have me up to their suite," said Owens. "But no one was going to offer me a job."

A laundry he owned went belly-up and he was forced to declare bankruptcy. One of the jobs that Owens took on was racing against horses, where he learned that the trick to staying with a high-strung

Thoroughbred was to have the starter as close as possible to the skittish animal. "It was bad enough to have toppled from the Olympic heights to make my living competing with animals," he said after racing a Thoroughbred named Julio McCaw at halftime of a soccer game. "But the competition wasn't even fair. No man could beat a racehorse, not even for 100 yards." Not even the great Jesse Owens.

#21

43 x 200

RICHARD PETTY IS NASCAR'S WINNINGEST
RACER WITH 200 VICTORIES

Richard Petty drives his 1969 Ford during a practice run in preparation for that year's Daytona 500.

"WHEN I FIRST STARTED RACING," RICHARD Petty once recalled, "one of the first things my father said was, 'Win the race as slow as you can.'" And over the course of more than 25 years, that's exactly what Lee Petty's son did. Two hundred times.

Petty started his career in 1958, just days after his 21st birthday, and won his first race in 1960, an untitled affair at the Southern States Fairgrounds near Charlotte. NASCAR was a much different sport back then, more of a barnstorming tour. The cars were much closer to stock than today's purpose-built racers, most of the tracks were half-mile and one-mile ovals, races were often held on weeknights, and the schedule often included more than one race per week.

Petty's best year was 1967, when he won an astonishing 27 of 48 races that season, including one stretch of 10 in a row. By comparison, 2005 season champ Tony Stewart won only five races. In Jeff Gordon's best season, he took the checkered flag only 13 times—less than half as often as Petty.

Petty's last win came on the Fourth of July in 1984, when he won the Firecracker 400, with President Ronald Reagan in attendance. And by this time, due in no small part to the man in the cowboy hat and the sunglasses, NASCAR had become a major national sport. Petty continued to race until 1992 and, ironically, his last race was the first race for a man who would inherit Petty's title as the circuit's top driver, Jeff Gordon.

THE DAYTONA 450

In 1974 Petty won the Daytona "450" after the race was shortened by 50 miles (20 laps) as a nod to America's ongoing energy crisis. NASCAR racers currently use an estimated 6,000 gallons of gas during a weekend of practice, qualifying, and a 500-mile race.

In between, Petty collected a record seven Daytona 500 wins and a record seven season points championships, a mark subsequently tied by the late Dale Earnhardt. More importantly, Petty was involved in many of the sport's most dramatic moments.

In 1976, Petty and David Pearson had been battling for the last 100 miles of the Daytona 500 race, and on the final lap Pearson's red and white Mercury managed to pass Petty's blue Dodge. Petty tried to return the favor, passing low but bumping Pearson in the process. Both cars crashed head-on into the wall and ultimately came to rest on the infield grass. Petty's car stalled—his crew would race out and push the disabled vehicle across the line illegally—but Pearson kept his car running, and he limped his damaged racer across the line for his only Daytona 500 victory.

Three years later, Petty would be the beneficiary of last-lap fireworks. Bobby Allison and Cale Yarborough were battling for the lead on the last lap of the 1979 Daytona 500 when Yarborough tried to pass. Allison blocked him; the resulting crash left the two cars stopped in the infield and the two drivers climbing out of their cars to wrestle in the muddy infield in front of a record television audience. Petty, who had been half a lap behind with mechanical trouble, swept past to take the checkered flag. This marquee moment is considered by many to be NASCAR's coming-out party as a national sport.

But the sport's first superstar set a record that will last as long as his legacy. Petty's 200 wins represent an unbreakable record. His nearest rival, Pearson, has 105 wins, just more than half of Petty's total. And no active driver has even an outside shot at the mark. With 73 wins as of the beginning of the 2006 season, Gordon will have to hustle to get halfway to Petty's record. Name any two stock car racing legends, add their wins together, and they won't even approach Petty's win total.

There's another number underpinning Petty's win total. He was able to compete in a remarkable 1,184 events—again, more than twice as many as those of his nearest rivals. Petty's career-winning percentage of 16.9 is actually lower than Pearson's (18.3 percent), and just about even with Gordon's (16.7 entering the 2006 season). So while Richard Petty has clearly earned the right to be called the king of stock car racing, what really set him apart was the length of his reign.

PETTY'S BEST YEAR WAS 1967, WHEN HE WON AN ASTONISHING 27 OF 48 RACES THAT SEASON, INCLUDING ONE STRETCH OF 10 IN A ROW. BY COMPARISON, 2005 SEASON CHAMP TONY STEWART WON ONLY FIVE RACES. IN JEFF GORDON'S BEST SEASON, HE TOOK THE CHECKERED FLAG 13 TIMES.

A FAMILY AFFAIR

Which family won the most NASCAR stock car races? It's not the Earnhardts, and no matter how many wins Dale Junior collects it's not likely to be enough to catch the Pettys. Patriarch Lee Petty won 54 races behind the wheel of his number 42 car. Richard, of course, added 200. And then Richard's son Kyle added eight more wins. Sadly, Kyle's son Adam was killed in practice for a race at Dover, New Hampshire, before he could get a chance to add to the family's victory total.

Richard Petty walks down pit row before the start of his 32nd and final Daytona 500 in 1992.

MISTER ROGERS'S NEIGHBORHOOD

IN 1924 ROGERS HORNSBY SET A RECORD FOR SINGLE-SEASON BATTING AVERAGE

WHILE EVERY BASEBALL FAN KNOWS THAT Ted Williams hit .406, how many remember the man who out-hit Teddy Ballgame by 18 points?

That would be Rogers Hornsby of the St. Louis Cardinals, who batted .424 in 1924, setting the modern record for highest batting average. Hornsby started off the 1924 season by going two-for-five against Vic Aldridge of the Cubs. Like so many other players through the years, he carried a .400 average after his first game. But in Hornsby's remarkable season, he would watch it go up from there.

Hornsby hit .429 in April, but in July he really got hot, with five three-hit games in a week. And in August the Rajah was *en fuego*. In the 10 games between August 20 and 26, which included three double-headers, Hornsby went 27 for 39, a sizzling .692 clip, with eight doubles, a triple, six homers, 16 runs scored, and a dozen runs batted in.

In back-to-back games on the 20th and 21st he went six for seven, then upped the ante, going seven for seven. For the month, Hornsby hit a cool .509. In September, Hornsby went into a full-fledged slump—at least by his own lofty standards. He hit only .352 and dropped his season average 10 points—from .434 to .424, which was still good enough to earn him his fifth straight batting title.

For the year, Hornsby struck out only 32 times. He also led the league in on-base percentage, slugging percentage, runs, hits, total bases, and doubles; and he finished second in home runs. Along with his .424 batting average, he had 227 hits, 121 runs scored, 43 doubles, 25 homers, and 94 RBIs.

But batting average is as batting average does. Despite Hornsby's heroics, the Cardinals finished in sixth place in an eight-team league, and attendance in St. Louis dropped by 19 percent. To add insult to injury, in the year he rewrote the record books, the MVP Award went to Dazzy Vance of the Brooklyn Robins, who won 28 games, compiled a 2.16 ERA, and struck out 262 batters. Was it personal? Probably. The outspoken Hornsby was universally disliked, a quality that continued into his old age.

"He couldn't carry my bat," he said about newly crowned home-run king Roger Maris. "He didn't hit in two years what I hit in one."

While some would point to Napoleon Lajoie's .426 average in 1901 as the modern record, it's easy to add an asterisk to that mark. That was the very first year of the American League, and the talent level was closer to minor league baseball than to the established National League. The 19th-century record belongs to Hugh Duffy, who hit .440 for the Boston Beaneaters in

Rogers Hornsby's .424 batting average for the Cardinals in 1924 is about as untouchable a mark as they come in the modern era. He batted nearly .700 during one exceptionally hot stretch in August that season.

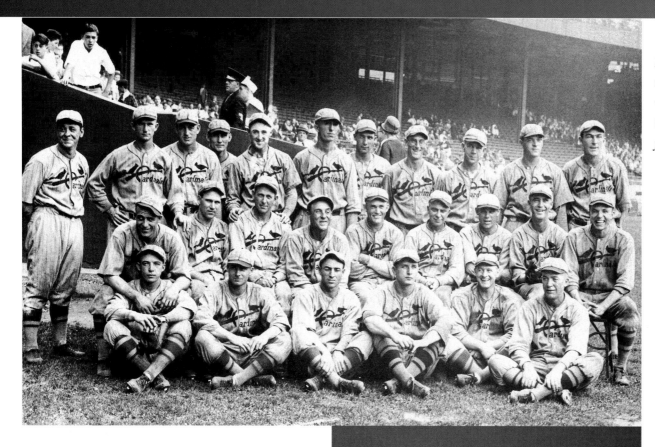

Hornsby, also the team's manager in this 1926 photo, was the centerpiece of the Cardinals (middle row, fifth from right).

THE WORLD ACCORDING TO HORNSBY

On hitting .424: "I hustled on everything I hit." On batting average: "Anyone who hits .250 doesn't belong in the major leagues." On pitchers: "I don't like to sound egotistical, but every time I stepped up to the plate with a bat in my hands, I couldn't help but feel sorry for the pitcher." On golf: "I don't play it. When I hit a ball, somebody else chases it."

1894. Although Hornsby set the record in 1924, some argue that his best season came in 1922, when he won the Triple Crown by hitting .401 with 42 homers and 152 RBIs.

While he made few friends in the game, there was little doubt that Rogers Hornsby could hit. Hornsby's .359 career average ranks second all-time to Ty Cobb's .366, and he hit a composite .402 for five seasons from 1921 to 1925.

Ted Williams said: "I've always felt Rogers Hornsby was the greatest hitter for average and power in the history of baseball."

"I'VE ALWAYS FELT ROGERS HORNSBY WAS THE GREATEST HITTER FOR AVERAGE AND POWER IN THE HISTORY OF BASEBALL."
—TED WILLIAMS

#23

THE MAN OF STEAL

RICKEY HENDERSON'S CAREER AND SINGLE-SEASON STOLEN-BASE RECORDS HAVE NEVER BEEN APPROACHED

Oakland's Rickey Henderson swipes his 119th base of the 1982 season, eclipsing the old mark previously held by Lou Brock. Henderson would finish the season with an amazing 130 stolen bases.

RICKEY HENDERSON IS THE GREATEST THIEF in the history of baseball. His 1,406 stolen bases far outstrip Lou Brock's old record of 938.

Playing for the Oakland A's in 1980 as a 21-year-old, Henderson became only the third player to steal 100 bases in a season. In 1982, with Billy Martin as his manager, Henderson had the green light for the whole season. He had an astonishing 82 bases by the All-Star break, an amazing total considering that since 1988, no player has stolen more than 84 in an entire season. On August 27, Henderson would break Lou Brock's record of 118 in style, stealing four bases in the game. He slowed his pace after breaking the record and ended the season with 130 steals. This record has never been seriously challenged, with only Vince Coleman even joining the 100-steal club since 1982. Henderson also set a record by being thrown out 42 times, but his 75 percent success rate was well above the break-even point.

And Henderson's presence on the base paths affected the whole game, with pitchers often paying more attention to Henderson on first than the hitter at the plate and throwing fastballs to give the catcher a fighting chance at throwing Rickey out at second. The so-called Rickey Rally marked an inning in which Henderson would walk, steal second, then steal third, and score on a sacrifice—all without the

> **"BILLY MARTIN WAS A GREAT FRIEND TO ME. I LOVE YOU, BILLY. I WISH YOU WERE HERE."**
>
> —RICKEY HENDERSON

SLIDE, BILLY, SLIDE

The greatest base-stealer of the 19th century was Sliding Billy Hamilton, who played for Kansas City, Philadelphia, and Boston between 1888 and 1901. The future Hall of Famer stole 912 bases, a total surpassed only by Henderson, Lou Brock, and Ty Cobb. His 1894 season, in which he scored 198 runs, still has never been surpassed. Hamilton's career .454 on-base percentage trails only Ted Williams, Babe Ruth, and John McGraw.

benefit of a hit. (In 2001 he broke the career record for walks, a mark previously held by Babe Ruth.) In 1983, Henderson would again break triple digits, with 108. Henderson would lead the league in steals a record 12 times, including one stretch of 11 times in 12 years.

These numbers made it a virtual certainty that he would break Lou Brock's career record, which he did on May 1, 1991, at the age of 32. His record-breaking moment came to be a touchstone of Henderson's largely undeserved public reputation. While hardly the Gettysburg Address, his speech stopped to thank—in order—God, the Haas family (owners of the Oakland A's), the organization, the city, "and all you beautiful fans for supporting me." Henderson continued by acknowledging his mother, friends, and loved ones; his first minor league manager, Tom Trebelhorn; and the late Billy Martin, who was his baseball mentor. "He was a great friend to me. I love you, Billy. I wish you were here." Rickey concluded with: "Lou Brock was the symbol of great base stealing, but today I am the greatest of all time. Thank you."

What his detractors latched on to was that last phrase, and Henderson was branded as egotistical and self-centered. It was only made worse when the eternally humble Nolan Ryan pitched a no-hitter that night. Henderson's aggressiveness on the base paths has not always made him friends. In a game in August 2001, Henderson stole second in the seventh inning with the Padres leading by a score of 12–5. Brewers manager Davey Lopes ran out of the dugout and went toe to toe with Henderson, a former teammate. "Stay in the game, and you're going down," Lopes warned.

"We're old school and there are some things that you just don't do," Lopes said later, ignoring the fact that he had done the same thing in the same situation several times in his career.

This focus on style rather than substance has made Henderson one of baseball's most underrated stars. When asked if he thought Rickey Henderson was a Hall of Fame–caliber player, baseball analyst Bill James responded, "If you could split him in half you'd have two Hall of Famers."

Henderson matched Brock with his career 938th stolen base in 1991, and a year later he became the only player ever to reach 1,000 career stolen bases.

#24 THE KINDEST CUTS

FOR SEVEN LONG YEARS, TIGER WOODS MADE EVERY PGA TOUR CUT

Tiger Woods had made 142 consecutive PGA tournament cuts, a string that extended seven years, before finally missing one on this day at the Byron Nelson Classic in Irving, Texas, on May 13, 2005.

THERE'S NO ROOM FOR ERROR IN GOLF. The slightest miscalculation in a swing or even an untimely gust of wind can take an approach shot that was headed for the center of the green and plop it down in the middle of a water hazard. A birdie try turns into a quadruple bogey. And a fight for the lead turns into a battle just to make the cut.

It's just that sort of disaster that Eldrick "Tiger" Woods was able to avoid for seven years. Woods, the holder of a piece of the scoring record at every major tournament, holds one of the most remarkable marks in the golf world: 142 consecutive tournaments without missing the cut.

This amazing string began in February of 1998 at the Buick Invitational. The week before, Woods withdrew from the Pebble Beach Pro-Am. He was four shots over par after two rounds of the 54-hole cut event. The final round of the tournament was postponed until August and Woods chose not to finish the event, which was to be concluded on the Monday after the PGA Championship. Before that, he had missed only one cut, at the 1997 Canadian Open where he bogeyed the final hole, shooting 70 and 76 and falling one stroke below the cut line.

Woods had already showed glimpses of his greatness with his record-breaking Masters win the previous spring. But 1998 would be an off-year, at least by

Woods's standards, as he redesigned his swing with the help of coach Butch Harmon, hoping to increase his consistency. And that he did and more. His next missed cut would not come until 2005. But he did have some severe tests of will over this amazing seven-year run.

In the 2001 PGA championship, Woods was two shots below the projected cut line on the back nine of the second round. In typical Tiger fashion, he rose to the occasion, sinking a 40-foot putt from off the green on the 15th and then drilling a 30-foot birdie putt on the 16th. Woods made the cut by a single stroke to keep the streak alive.

In the 2003 Masters, he was again on the ropes on the back nine during the second round. He birdied

A KINDER CUT

The all-time mark in consecutive cuts made is by LPGA golfer Jane Blalock: a remarkable 299 in a row. The streak started in her rookie season of 1969 and ran through the last event of the 1980 season. Blalock retired at the height of her game in 1986 with 29 victories to her credit—one short of the number required for automatic induction into the LPGA Hall of Fame.

number 7, his 16th hole of the round, and seemed to be safe. But on number 8, needing a two putt from 25 feet for par, Woods three-jacked for a bogey and fell back to five over and right on the cut line. His last hole of the round didn't start out auspiciously. He misfired a drive into the trees, punched out into a greenside bunker, managed to work his ball out of the trap to within three feet, and sank the par putt to make the cut on the number. A not-so-routine par with a five-year consecutive cut streak on the line? Just another day at the office for Tiger Woods.

Later that year he would tie Byron Nelson's consecutive record of 113 at the Funai Classic, then break it at the Tour Championships in November. At the 2005 EDS Byron Nelson Classic, on May 13, 2005, the stage was set yet again for another Tiger Miracle and another clutch finish to keep the streak alive. Tiger came to the final hole of the second round needing par to make the cut. After hitting a 7 iron in the bunker for his second shot, he had to get up and down to play the weekend. He blasted out of the sand to about 15 feet. The stage was set for another clutch moment from Woods. All eyes were on him.

"Every guy in the locker room was watching," said Jesper Parnevik. "We were not allowed to bet, but guys were offering $1,000 he would make it."

And he almost always did. But not this time. Tiger lined up for the putt and the ball trickled an inch past the hole. Woods tapped in for bogey, leaving him outside the cut line.

"I just tried to bandage my way to the finish," Woods said philosophically. "I just didn't quite have

it." The streak lasted seven years, three months, and seven days.

To put Woods's amazing—and some think unbreakable—streak in perspective, when Tiger started the streak NBA superstar LeBron James had just turned 14, and women's golfer Michelle Wie was just seven years old. Yes, seven. Or consider this. Entering the 2006 season, the longest active streak on the Tour belonged to Ernie Els. He had made only 20 cuts in a row, less than a season's worth.

Woods's streak began in February 1998, a week after he withdrew from the Pebble Beach Pro-Am while sitting at four over par after two rounds.

Woods had several close calls during his unbelievable streak, but in typical fashion, he almost always managed to get himself out of trouble when it appeared he was doomed to miss a cut.

"I JUST TRIED TO BANDAGE MY WAY TO THE FINISH. I JUST DIDN'T QUITE HAVE IT."
—TIGER WOODS, AFTER MISSING HIS FIRST CUT IN MORE THAN SEVEN YEARS

OR DID HE?

While the PGA Tour recognizes Tiger Woods's streak at 142, some critics, such as former USGA president Frank Hannigan, disagree. He argues that the streak shouldn't count "no-cut" events, such as the Accenture Match Play and Tour Championships. Eliminate the no-cut events and Woods's streak stops at 111, two short of Byron Nelson's. The PGA Tour defends their inclusion because their threshold for making the cut is "picking up a check," which Woods did in those events. Perhaps in response to this criticism, Woods marks the beginning of the streak differently than the PGA Tour does, suggesting that the streak extends back to the Disney World Oldsmobile Classic in 1997. "I don't care what the PGA Tour thinks, I didn't miss the cut at the 1998 AT&T Pebble Beach Pro-Am; I withdrew," says Woods on his Web site. (Woods was among 43 players who didn't return for the final round.) Of course, there's also the question of the record-keeping in Nelson's time. Many of the events didn't have 36-hole cuts, and some that did offered prize money only to the top 20 finishers, putting a wrinkle in the PGA Tour's "get a check/make the cut" policy.

#25 THE MIRACLE MILE

THEY SAID IT COULDN'T BE DONE, BUT ROGER BANNISTER'S FOUR-MINUTE MILE PROVED THEM WRONG

Britain's Roger Bannister, a 25-year-old medical student, hits the tape to break the elusive four-minute mile in Oxford, England, on May 6, 1954.

"**DOCTORS AND SCIENTISTS SAID THAT** breaking the four-minute mile was impossible, that one would die in the attempt," said Roger Bannister. "Thus, when I got up from the track after collapsing at the finish line, I figured I was dead."

On May 6, 1954, the 25-year-old medical student did the impossible, recording a time of 3:59.4 at the Iffley Road track in Oxford, where Bannister was studying.

For almost two decades the four-minute mile had been an elusive goal, tantalizing runners who came close but never quite broke it. Between 1931 and 1934 the mile record fell from 4:09.2 to 4:06.8. In the early 1940s, two Swedes, Gunder Hagg and Arne Andersson, lowered the record six times between them with Hagg running a 4:01.4 in July 1945 to edge Anderson's 1944 record of 4:01.6.

And that's where the record stayed for almost a decade, with each unsuccessful attempt making the four-minute barrier seem that much more formidable.

Leading up to his record run, Bannister was not your conventional track star. At the 1952 Helsinki Games, he finished a disappointing fourth in the 1,500-meter run, so he turned his attention to the four-minute mile. However, he was also beginning medical school full time, so he allotted himself only an hour a day for training. He would take a 10-minute

THE EXTRA MILE

The world record for running the mile has been broken no fewer than 18 times by 13 different runners since Bannister toppled the four-minute mark. The current record, as of May 2006, was 3:43.13 set by Hicham El Guerrouj of Morocco on July 7, 1999. The women's world record is 4:12.56 by Svetlana Masterkova of Russia on August 14, 1996.

jog over to the track, run 10 400-meter sprints, and jog back, leaving him just enough time to wolf down his lunch.

Bannister was locked in a battle with John Landy of Australia, who also had his sights set on the mark. On a grass track, in December 1952, Landy ran a 4:02.1, the fastest time since Hagg. A month later he was under a four-minute pace until fading in the last 20 seconds. In another record attempt, he ran half the race with a stray football cleat piercing his foot through his thin track spikes.

Relieved that Landy wasn't able to break the record before the end of Australia's outdoor track season, Bannister was closing in himself. Eleven months before his landmark win, Bannister set a British mile record of 4:02, but the time was disallowed by the British Amateur Athletic Board because he used pacesetters. "In the 1950s, pacemaking was strictly illegal," wrote John Bryant in his book, *3:59.4*. "No athlete was supposed to enter a race unless he intended to complete it and try to win it." Chris Brasher ran so slowly during the early stages of the race that Bannister lapped him, and he paced Bannister on his final lap, actually shouting encouragement. Bannister was hardly the first runner to use these methods: Hagg had pacesetting help from a teammate who dropped out of the race during his world record run. On Bannister's record attempt, Brasher and Christopher Chataway were clearly supporting Bannister, but did so in a less obvious way. When the gun went off, Brasher was actually called for a very rare false start, underscoring the tension on the track. Brasher led for the first two laps before falling back. Chataway took over and led the race until the last half of the last lap. Chataway was slowing, but Bannister kept to his plan and stayed behind until the final straightaway. Bannister sprinted to the line, and the image of the young Briton hurling himself at the tape is one of the classic sports images of all time. "It's the ability to take more out of yourself than you've got," he said later.

While Bannister earned international fame with the record, he wasn't the only one who made a name for himself. Two years later, Brasher would win the gold medal in the 3,000-meter steeplechase and Chataway would go on to set the world record in the 5,000 meters. The timekeeper of the day, Norris McWhirter, would go on to become the editor of the *Guinness Book of World Records*.

Once Bannister broke the record, the four-minute barrier didn't seem so formidable anymore. Landy shattered Bannister's world record only a month later with a time of 3:58.0. Bannister would race against Landy in the Commonwealth Games in a much-hyped faceoff called the Mile of the Century. Both runners

Bannister (329) and Australian John Landy compete in the first mile race in history in which two runners finish in under four minutes. Bannister clocked in at 3:58.8 and Landy at 3:59.6, on August 7, 1954.

TWO BY FOUR

After the four-minute mile, what do you do for an encore? How about two in a row? On July 19, 1997, in Hechtel, Belgium, Kenyan runner Daniel Komen ran two miles in under eight minutes. Komen ran the first mile in 3:59.2 and the second in 3:59.4, bettering Bannister's milestone pace.

would break four minutes, and Bannister would prevail, clocking a 3:58.8, with Landy just behind at 3:59.6. Bannister became the first recipient of the now-coveted *Sports Illustrated* Sportsman of the Year Award and retired later that year to concentrate on his studies.

"DOCTORS AND SCIENTISTS SAID THAT BREAKING THE FOUR-MINUTE MILE WAS IMPOSSIBLE, THAT ONE WOULD DIE IN THE ATTEMPT. THUS, WHEN I GOT UP FROM THE TRACK AFTER COLLAPSING AT THE FINISH LINE, I FIGURED I WAS DEAD."
—ROGER BANNISTER

HITS AND MISSES

PETE ROSE BROKE A GREAT RECORD,
BUT IS THAT ENOUGH TO MAKE HIM GREAT?

CAN YOU OWN A GREAT RECORD WITHOUT being a great player? That's the question that needs to be asked about Pete Rose. He holds one of baseball's most hallowed records, the all-time hits mark previously held by Ty Cobb. Any way you look at it, the all-time hits record is an impressive one. Ty Cobb is one of the game's great players, and arguably its greatest hitter.

Over the years, 3,000 hits has become a classic milestone, an automatic ticket to Cooperstown. Until Pete Rose, Cobb was the only hitter to pass the next round number and collect 4,000 hits. Rose joined the 3,000-hit club in May of 1978 at the age of 37, the same year he set a National League record with his 44-game hitting streak. He then set his sights squarely on Cobb.

After signing as a free agent with the Phillies, Rose hooked up with the Expos, and then returned to the Reds for his ill-fated gig as player/manager, where in addition to any extracurricular activities, he cost his team games by writing his name in the lineup instead of those of such talented young players as Eric Davis and Kal Daniels.

It took him more than seven seasons to finally collect the record. The date was September 11, 1986, and Rose hit an Eric Show slider into left center field at Riverfront Stadium for a single and a place in the record book. He would continue to play for another season and run the record up to 4,256.

"When I get the record, all it will make me is the player with the most hits," said Rose, during his pursuit. "I'm also the player with the most at-bats and the most outs. I never said I was a greater player than (Ty) Cobb."

But is he a better player than, say, Tim Raines? Sure, Rose has a huge edge in hits—1,651 to be exact. Rose has a tiny edge in batting average—.303 to .294, but Raines tops him in on-base percentage (.385 to .375). He tops him in slugging percentage (.425 to .409). Raines has more home runs (170 to 160). Then look at the stolen base totals. Raines has 808 stolen bases to Rose's 198. But Rose was actually thrown out trying to steal more often than Raines was (149 to 146).

With a 57 percent stolen-base average, well below the acknowledged break-even point of 66 percent, Pete Rose was actually hurting his teams with his aggressiveness on the basepaths. Charlie Hustle hustled too much. The comparison isn't between Rose and Raines, who was an all-star but has never been a serious Hall of Fame candidate, but with other players in baseball's pantheon.

And once you get past that gaudy hit total, Rose didn't bring much else to the party in terms of walks, power, or speed. For example, his OPS of .784 is the

Pete Rose breaks Ty Cobb's all-time career hits record with this single off of San Diego pitcher Eric Show on September 11, 1985.

> "WHEN I GET THE RECORD, ALL IT WILL MAKE ME IS THE PLAYER WITH THE MOST HITS. I'M ALSO THE PLAYER WITH THE MOST AT-BATS AND THE MOST OUTS. I NEVER SAID I WAS A GREATER PLAYER THAN (TY) COBB."
> —PETE ROSE

same as Johnny Damon's entering the 2006 season, and big contract or no, few consider Damon a future Hall of Famer. So in a purely rational universe, the question of whether Pete Rose belongs in the Hall of Fame would center not on the off-the-field activities that resulted in his being barred from baseball, but on his very real shortcomings as a player. Rose's record is more a testament to his persistence than transcendent skill.

But what he did well was lace them up. Rose had 14,053 at-bats, 1,689 more than Hank Aaron, who's second on the list. He played more major league games than anyone in history, 3,562, which is 254 more than Carl Yastrzemski had. So while over the years Pete Rose has given his fans plenty of reasons to doubt his word, when he says "I'd walk through hell in a gasoline suit to play baseball," you have to believe him.

Rose fights off tears after collecting his 4,192nd career base hit to surpass the immortal Ty Cobb for one of baseball's longest-standing records.

TWO HITS TOO MANY

Many, including former commissioner Fay Vincent and investigator John Dowd, have argued that the inclusion of Rose's record-breaking bat and ball in the Baseball Hall of Fame's collection is honor enough. But it turns out that Cooperstown probably has the wrong artifacts. A careful accounting of Ty Cobb's hit totals by historian Pete Palmer revealed that two hits in 1910 were double-counted. Commissioner Bowie Kuhn declared that "the statute of limitation" had expired and refused to change Cobb's hit total. However, recent editions of *Total Baseball*, once considered baseball's official record book, have revised the old record downward from 4,191 to 4,189. That means that Rose actually broke Cobb's record on September 8, 1986, with a single off Cubs right-hander Reggie Patterson.

#27 MATCHING SETS

FOR ALMOST AN ENTIRE TENNIS SEASON, MARTINA NAVRATILOVA WAS UNBEATABLE

During an unbelievable stretch during the 1984 season—a span that would continue for 10 months—Martina Navratilova was unbeatable, winning 74 consecutive matches.

THERE'S A REASON WINNING A TENNIS match is one of the hardest feats in sports. In tennis, there are no timeouts, no substitutions, and there's no running out the clock or being saved by the bell. If you want to walk off the court with a smile on your face, you've got no other choice. You've got to find a way to win that last point. And during a magical 10-month period in 1984, Martina Navratilova accomplished that daunting feat, again and again.

The Hall of Famer won 74 consecutive matches, easily eclipsing the previous record of 55 set by Chris Evert in 1974. After defecting from the Czech Republic in the mid-1970s, and flirting with both excellence (winning Wimbledon) and excess (American fast food), Navratilova brought the women's game kicking and screaming into the modern day. She approached the formerly genteel sport with single-mindedness. She assembled a bevy of experts called Team Navratilova to help raise the level of her game. She remade her once-pudgy body, becoming the fittest player on tour. And her superiority was never more apparent than during her classic 1984 season.

Navratilova's remarkable winning streak started at the U.S. Indoors in East Hanover, New Jersey, with a first round 6–3, 6–2 win over Nancy Yeargin. She won 13 tournaments in a row, including the French Open, Wimbledon, and the U.S. Open. While there were

Navratilova's feat easily eclipsed the previous mark of 55 straight victories accomplished by Chris Evert (left).

"WHOEVER SAID 'IT'S NOT WHETHER YOU WIN OR
LOSE THAT COUNTS' PROBABLY LOST."
—MARTINA NAVRATILOVA

certainly any number of easy matches, straight-set wins over players like Ann Kiyomura and Bonnie Gadusek, Navratilova also faced some of the sport's legends. For example, she defeated Chris Evert-Lloyd six times during the season, including in all three Grand Slam finals. She lost only seven sets during the streak, two to Evert-Lloyd, two to Hana Mandlikova, and one each to Pam Shriver, Claudia Kohde-Kilsch, and Cathy Rinaldi.

Navratilova's streak finally ended in the semifinals of the Australian Open on December 6, 1984, with a 1–6, 6–3, 7–5 loss to Helena Sukova. That match actually derailed a much more significant date with destiny. If she had gone on to capture the title at the Australian, which was then the last major of the year, Navratilova—who won six majors in a row, but not in the same calendar year—would have captured the coveted singles Grand Slam, the only major feat that eluded her during her career.

Over the next three years Navratilova's dominance would continue. She would reach the finals of all 11 Grand Slam tournaments that she would enter and win six of them. All in all, she would win a record 167 singles titles, including 18 Grand Slam titles.

Navratilova's streak is longer than the record men's streak of 50 held by Guillermo Vilas. Vilas's unbeaten string ended in controversial fashion when he faced Ilie Nastase, who was using the soon-to-be illegal spaghetti racket. Vilas quit the match in disgust.

The streak is also longer than the longest unbeaten marks in team sports: a 33-game streak by the Los Angeles Lakers, a 26-game streak by the New York Giants, a 21-game streak by the New England

STILL SLAMMING

Still active, Navratilova continues to rewrite the record books. In 2003, at age 46 years and eight months, she won the Wimbledon mixed doubles with Leander Paes to become the oldest player to win a Grand Slam title and tied Billie Jean King for the most Wimbledon titles with 20. Her total of Grand Slams is 58, second only to Margaret Court's 62. In 2004 Navratilova became the oldest woman in 82 years to win a singles match at Wimbledon.

Patriots, and a 17-game skein by the Pittsburgh Penguins.

During her 21-year Hall of Fame career, Navratilova set any number of records. Her 167 singles titles, including 18 Grand Slams, is more than any other player's, man or woman. From 1982 to 1984, when her lefty serve-and-volley game was at its best, Navratilova's record was a mind-blowing 254–6. But her most enduring legacy and most unbreakable mark was that classic winning streak, set by the sport's most tenacious competitor.

As Navratilova once quipped, "Whoever said 'It's not whether you win or lose that counts' probably lost."

As impressive as her 74-match streak in singles was, Navratilova actually one-upped herself on the doubles court, winning an incredible 109 straight matches with partner Pam Shriver from 1982 to 1984.

DOUBLE YOUR PLEASURE

The 74-match winning streak was actually the second longest of Navratilova's career. Between 1983 and 1985, Navratilova and her partner Pam Shriver put together an astonishing 109-match streak. While some would argue that Navratilova is the greatest singles player of all time, her claim to supremacy in doubles is even stronger. She won 40 Grand Slam doubles titles, 31 in women's doubles and nine in mixed doubles.

#28

FAST MONEY

FORMULA ONE RACER MICHAEL SCHUMACHER IS NOT ONLY THE WORLD'S FASTEST ATHLETE, HE'S THE RICHEST, TOO

Michael Schumacher, the world's highest-paid athlete, steers his Formula One race car into a curve during the 2004 Belgian Grand Prix.

WHO IS THE HIGHEST-PAID ATHLETE IN THE WORLD? It's not A-Rod or Shaq or Peyton Manning. That distinction belongs to Formula One racer Michael Schumacher, who drives for the Ferrari team and makes an estimated $40 million for driving in 18 races, according to *Forbes* magazine.

That's straight guaranteed salary, which dwarfs Alex Rodriguez's $25 million. Schumacher can add between $20 and $40 million to that figure with endorsement income. While he's virtually unknown in America, the German driver is a huge international star, ranking 17th on the *Forbes* Celebrity 100, ahead of Jay Leno, P-Diddy, and Jennifer Lopez.

THE MONEY SPENT ON A DRIVER LIKE SCHUMACHER WHO CAN GET THE ADVERTISER'S LOGO ON WORLDWIDE TELEVISION IN THE WORLD'S SECOND-MOST-POPULAR SPORT (BEHIND SOCCER) IS WELL JUSTIFIED.

Given the exorbitant costs of running a Formula One team—the top teams like Ferrari can spend $400 million per season—the money spent on a driver like Schumacher, who can get the advertiser's logo on worldwide television in the world's second-most-popular sport (behind soccer), is well justified.

"He is incredibly professional," said former world champion Damon Hill. "If you had to go for a heart operation, you'd want somebody who was the Schumacher of the heart surgery world to do the job, because you can rely on him."

And Schumacher is clearly worth the money. At his best, he is nearly perfect.

In 2004, for example, Schumacher won the first five races of the season. At the Monaco Grand Prix he failed to finish after a controversial accident with Juan Pablo Montoya during a caution period following another crash. Schumacher went on to win the next seven races for an unprecedented string of 12 of 13 wins, breaking his own single season record of 11 wins in a season, set in 2002.

The winning streak was broken at the Belgian Grand Prix, where Schumacher finished a close second behind Kimi Raikkonen of Finland in a McLaren. At the Italian Grand Prix, Schumacher again finished second, this time behind teammate Rubens Barrichello, a loss largely viewed as a gesture of gratitude to a loyal teammate. In Japan, Schumacher recorded his record-breaking 13th win in an 18-race schedule, breaking his own record by

winning a seventh world championship—his fifth in a row. By any statistical measure, Schumacher is the greatest Formula One driver of all time.

As of the beginning of the 2006 season, he had 84 wins, far outpacing the 51 wins of previous record holder Alain Prost. Until Schumacher came along, Formula One racing was quite the competitive affair. Between 1960 and 1985, no driver was able to manage back-to-back championships, and the record of the great Argentine driver Juan Manuel Fangio of five titles, including four in a row during the 1950s, was largely thought to be unbreakable.

Schumacher owns almost every important record in the sport—he owns career records for total points, podiums, fastest laps, races led, laps led, and second-place finishes, and the longest span between his first and last wins. As of the beginning of the 2006 season, Schumacher was closing in on the one major record that he didn't hold, the record for career pole positions by the late Ayrton Senna.

While most of Schumacher's records are well out of reach—at least for the near future—his salary mark is likely to be broken sooner rather than later. Senna was his predecessor as the world's highest-paid athlete, and it's likely that when the 35-year old German retires, his place at the top of the all-time salary charts will be taken by his heir apparent, possibly Raikkonen or 2005 world champion Fernando Alonzo.

CRASH COURSES

Early in his career Schumacher found himself involved in several controversial finishes. In 1994 he crashed into top-rival Damon Hill in the final laps of the season-ending Australian Grand Prix. The accident put both cars out of the race but gave the championship to Schumacher. In the Spanish Grand Prix of 1997, Jacques Villeneuve tried to pass Schumacher for the lead, and Schumacher turned into him to keep the Canadian from taking the lead. Villeneuve limped home to take the win and the World Championship, and Schumacher was stripped of his points for the year and his second-place rank in the season championship.

COMMERCIAL ZONE

While Michael Schumacher tops all athletes with his $40 million salary, when you add in endorsement income, Tiger Woods takes over the top spot, according to a June 2005 *Forbes* magazine study.

1. Tiger Woods	$87M
2. Michael Schumacher	$60M
3. Oscar De La Hoya	$38M
4. Michael Vick	$37.5M
5. Shaquille O'Neal	$33.4M
6. Michael Jordan	$33M
7. David Beckham	$32.5M
8. Kobe Bryant	$28.8M
T-9. Lance Armstrong	$28M
T-9. Valentino Rossi	$28M

Schumacher raises his trophy after winning the Australian Grand Prix in Melbourne on March 12, 2000.

#29 THE LONGEST YARDS

QB DAN MARINO PASSED FOR MILES
MORE THAN HIS NEAREST COMPETITOR

WHAT WOULD YOU RATHER DO, SET THE all-time record for touchdown passes or win a Super Bowl? What would you rather do, set the all-time record for pass completions or win a Super Bowl? What would you rather do, set the all-time record for yardage or win a Super Bowl?

In the end, this is how history will remember Dan Marino. The Dolphins quarterback did everything you could do while throwing the football—including tossing for nearly 10,000 yards more than his nearest competitor—but he never won a championship.

The record book says that Marino is the best passer of all time. When he retired he owned 23 NFL marks and shared five others. The most impressive? In a career that stretched from 1983 to 1999, he threw for an astonishing 61,361 yards—9,886 yards more than second-place John Elway.

The Dolphins were able to secure Marino with the number 27 pick of the 1983 draft. He had enjoyed a fine career at Pittsburgh—his hometown university—but his senior season had been a bit rocky. Rumors about his dedication surfaced and his stock plummeted on draft day. Marino was the sixth quarterback picked in the first round, after John Elway, Todd Blackledge, Jim Kelly, Tony Eason, and Ken O'Brien.

When he was finished, the Dolphins' Dan Marino had passed for an unprecedented 61,361 yards, nearly 10,000 more than friendly rival and second-place holder John Elway.

> "YOU WERE BASICALLY AT DAN'S MERCY. ALL THE GREAT ONES SEE THE GAME
> SO QUICKLY THAT WHEN EVERYBODY ELSE IS RUNNING AROUND LIKE A CHICKEN
> WITH HIS HEAD CUT OFF, THEY KNOW EXACTLY WHERE THEY WANT
> TO GO WITH THE BALL. IT'S LIKE THEY SEE EVERYTHING IN SLOW MOTION."
> —49ERS HALL OF FAME DEFENSIVE BACK RONNIE LOTT

"We didn't even work him out," Don Shula recalled. "He had too much talent to go that low. But somehow he did, and we were more than happy to bring him in."

With his quick release, arm strength, and sensational accuracy, Marino would become an overnight success.

In his sophomore season of 1984, he threw for a record 5,084 yards and a then-record 48 TD passes. "You were basically at Dan's mercy," said San Francisco's Ronnie Lott, the Hall of Fame defensive back. "All the great ones see the game so quickly that when everybody else is running around like a chicken with his head cut off, they know exactly where they want to go with the ball. It's like they see everything in slow motion."

That season Marino led the Dolphins to a 14–2 season and a berth in Super Bowl XIX. A one-sided 38–16 loss was as close as Marino would ever get to a ring, with Joe Montana, who would throw for 147 fewer regular-season touchdowns than Marino, collecting his second of four Super Bowl rings.

For his part, Marino would never even get back to the big game. "I'd trade every record we broke to be Super Bowl champs," he would say.

IMMORTALIZED IN BRONZE

Before he was inducted into the Pro Football Hall of Fame, Dan Marino was honored by the Miami Dolphins. In 2000 they retired his No. 13 jersey, the second such honor by the franchise after Bob Griese. A life-size bronze statue of Marino stands outside Dolphin Stadium, and Stadium Street, a road near the complex, was renamed Dan Marino Drive.

OF ORWELL AND MARINO

Take nothing away from the 49 TD passes that Peyton Manning threw in 2004, but Dan Marino's 1984 season is probably the greatest year that any pro quarterback has ever had. In just his second year, he became the only quarterback to ever throw for more than 5,000 yards, a record that stands to this day. The MVP-to-be opened the season with five touchdown passes and ended it by tossing four in each of the final four games. Marino completed 362 of 564 attempts and averaged 318 yards a game. He pummeled opposing secondaries with 48 TD passes—an average of three a game—a total that beat the previous record held by Y. A. Tittle and George Blanda, by 12. "There were times on the field when I felt like I couldn't miss that season," said Marino. "The ball was always on time, it was always catchable, and I was making the right decisions on who to throw to."

Marino celebrates after breaking Fran Tarkenton's record for career passing yards in a game against the New England Patriots on November 12, 1995.

#30 GETTING ON

TED WILLIAMS REACHED BASE
BETTER THAN ANY HITTER IN HISTORY

TED BALLGAME IN THE AIR

After receiving much public criticism when he received a draft deferment in 1942, Williams did an about-face and joined the marines. He didn't see action during World War II, but during the Korean War he flew 39 missions as a marine fighter pilot and was almost shot down on at least two occasions. After his baseball career was over, Williams was inducted into the Fishing Hall of Fame.

BASEBALL IS A GAME OF DISAPPOINTMENT. Every Major League hitter must resign himself to one thing—that he will fail more often than he succeeds. He will walk dejectedly back to the dugout more often than he will touch first safely.

Over the course of his career, the player who came closest to turning that immutable law of the diamond on its head was Ted Williams. The great Red Sox slugger posted a career on-base percentage of .482, which means that 48.2 percent of the time, he did what he set out to do—get on base.

Although it was invented by Branch Rickey, on-base percentage has become the ultimate new-school baseball stat. It was first popularized by such sabermetricians as Bill James, who realized that batting averages didn't tell the whole story. Then organizations like Billy Beane's Oakland A's adopted it as a way to gain an advantage. And OBP finally reached mainstream popularity with Michael Lewis's best-selling *Moneyball*.

But if you want to see the power of patience in action, look no further than Ted Williams. His .344 career batting average was good enough for seventh all time, but what made him perhaps the greatest hitter of all time was his batting eye. Williams's career walk percentage was .207, which meant that he was flirting with the Mendoza Line without even swinging the bat.

There's no doubt that Williams possessed tremendous physical gifts—such as his 20/10 eyesight—but he coupled that with an utterly uncompromising approach to hitting. Williams resolutely refused to swing at anything out of the strike zone, which forced pitchers to throw him strikes, often with devastating results. Pitcher Bobby Shantz neatly summed up the pitcher's conundrum. "He won't hit anything bad. But don't give him anything good."

Feasting on the good stuff that pitchers were forced to throw, the ever-patient Williams won six batting titles and led the league in slugging nine times. But it was one stat, on-base percentage, that was the private province of the Splendid Splinter. Between 1940 and 1958, Williams led the league in on-base percentage in every year in which he played enough to be eligible, 12 times in all.

In three of those years, Williams pulled off one of baseball's most singular feats. He posted an on-base percentage of over .500, which means that he got on more often than he made an out. In 1941, the year he hit .406, he also recorded a then-record .553 on-base percentage. In 1954, his OBP was .513, and in 1957 he posted a .532 mark.

How rare is it to turn the game upside down like this? Only four other players since 1901 have managed it. Rogers Hornsby pulled it off once, registering a .507

OBP in 1924. Mickey Mantle did it once, with a .512 OBP in 1957. The great Babe Ruth did it five times between 1920 and 1926. And Barry Bonds has done it four times. In 2002 he broke Williams's single-season record with a .582 on-base percentage. Two years later, he posted a mind-boggling .609 OBP, combining a .362 batting average with an unbelievable 232 walks.

But for all Bonds's recent heroics, in career on-base percentage he still ranks well behind Teddy Ballgame. "When I walk down the street and meet people," Ted Williams once said, "I just want them to think 'There goes the greatest hitter who ever lived.'" If you believe the game's most important stat, Theodore Samuel Williams might have achieved just that.

Ted Williams singles in his first at-bat of a 1954 doubleheader, in which he went eight-for-nine with two home runs.

> "HE WON'T HIT ANYTHING BAD.
>   BUT DON'T GIVE HIM ANYTHING GOOD."
> —OPPOSING PITCHER BOBBY SHANTZ

I AM A CAMERA

Williams aside, who's the most purely patient hitter in baseball history? That would have to be Max "Camera Eye" Bishop. The second baseman played 12 seasons for the Philadelphia A's and the Boston Red Sox from 1924 to 1935, and he "walked" at a .204 pace, better than Babe Ruth and just behind Ted Williams. Why haven't you ever heard of him? Because he couldn't do much else. His career batting average was only .271, he was caught stealing more times than he swiped successfully, and his career high in home runs was 10. Bishop was the leadoff man on the Connie Mack A's of the early 1930s, widely considered one of the greatest teams of all time, and he set the table ahead of Al Simmons, Mickey Cochrane, and Jimmie Foxx. In 1930 he became the only everyday player in modern baseball history to have more runs scored (117) than hits (111) in a season. His .423 career on-base percentage would have made him a star in today's "Moneyball" game, but 80 years ago, it did nothing more than earn him a colorful nickname.

Whether he was hitting home runs, as he did in this final at-bat of his legendary career, or taking walks, Williams's on-base percentage is perhaps the most striking of all of his accomplishments.

31

THE GOLDEN GAMES

MARK SPITZ'S SEVEN GOLD MEDALS IN
1972 SET AN ENDURING OLYMPIC RECORD

PHELPS'S FAILED ATTEMPT

In the 2004 Athens Olympics, American swimmer Michael Phelps took aim at Spitz's record by entering eight events. He won his first race, the 100-meter butterfly, but his quest was derailed in his second race, the 200-meter freestyle, when he finished third behind Ian Thorpe. Phelps won the rest of his individual events, but the U.S. finished third in the 4 x 100–meter freestyle relay. His total medal haul was six golds and two bronzes.

SOMETIMES, SWIMMING WELL IS THE BEST revenge. At the 1968 Olympics, Mark Spitz predicted, Namath-style, that he would come home with six gold medals. His haul of two gold, one silver, and a bronze would have made the average Olympian ecstatic, but Spitz returned home from Mexico City thinking he had failed.

Four years later at the 1972 Munich Games, Spitz showed in no uncertain terms why he wasn't your average athlete. He became the first and only athlete to win seven gold medals in a single Olympiad. To top off his perfect run, he set a world record in all seven events. He won four individual medals—the 100- and 200-meter freestyle and the 100- and 200-meter butterfly—and three relay races: the 4 x 100 and 4 x 200–meter freestyle relay and the 4 x 100–meter medley.

Even more astonishingly, all the world records he broke in his individual events were his own.

Here's a brief rundown of Spitz's Golden Games.

The 200-meter butterfly: in his first race, Spitz finished two seconds faster than second-place finisher American Gary Hall Jr. and six seconds better than the fastest previous Olympic 200 butterfly time. "I take credit for setting the tone," said his Olympic roommate, Hall. Spitz swam a 2:00.70, shattering his own world record of 2:01.53, set 26 days earlier.

The 400-meter freestyle relay: only an hour after his first, Spitz won his second gold medal as his team,

Mark Spitz acknowledges the cheers at the Munich Olympic Games of 1972 after winning his fourth gold medal of the Games, setting a world record in the 100-meter butterfly.

Spitz competes in the 400-meter medley in Munich on September 4, 1972, pacing the American team to the gold medal with a world-record time of 3:48.16.

which included Dave Edgar, Jerry Heidenreich, and John Murphy, finished in 3:26.42, well under the previous world record time set earlier that same day by another team of Americans (3:28.84).

The 200-meter freestyle: American Steve Genter led this race at the final turn, but Spitz turned it on at the finish and won by less than a second. He finished with a world-record time of 1:52.78, topping his old world-record time of 1:53.5. He defeated teammate Steve Genter, who had been hospitalized only days before with a collapsed lung.

After the race, Spitz stirred some controversy by waving his Adidas sneakers to the crowd. IOC officials, among others, suspected Spitz of trying to endorse his sponsor's product, a no-no at the then–strictly amateur Olympics. Spitz maintained he was expressing his enthusiasm over his third gold medal and nothing more. "I'm already Jesse Owens. Now

they're trying to make a Jim Thorpe out of me," said Spitz, who got off with a warning from the IOC.

The 100-meter butterfly: in Spitz's favorite event, he completed the race in 54.27, beating his own world record of 54.56. His winning margin over Canadian Bruce Robertson was 1.3 seconds, or about a body length. Spitz had owned the record since 1967, when he beat the five-year-old mark set by Luis Nicolao of Argentina. Spitz would break his own record six times in five years, shaving $2^{1}/_{2}$ seconds off Nicolao's record. His fourth gold in the games tied the U.S. record set by American sprinter Jesse Owens in Berlin in 1936, and swimmer Don Schollander, who won four gold medals at Tokyo in 1964.

The 4 x 200–meter relay: less than an hour later, Spitz helped the U.S. secure yet another gold medal, swimming the anchor leg. With a time of 7:35.78 he and his teammates had lowered the world record time of 7:43.3, which Spitz had set with three other U.S. swimmers, by more than seven seconds. His fifth gold tied the record set by Italian fencer Nedo Nadi, who won his at Antwerp in 1920.

The 100-meter freestyle: the most memorable race of those Olympics is the one he almost didn't compete in. Why was he almost a no-show? The most common explanation was that the 100-meter freestyle was Spitz's weakest discipline and he feared losing to fellow American Jerry Heidenreich, who had posted a quicker time in his leg of the team freestyle relay.

Prior to the event, Spitz had said, "I'd rather win six out of six, or even four out of four, then six out of seven. It's reached a point to where my self-esteem comes into it. I just don't want to lose."

THE FLOW OF PROGRESS

Spitz attempted a comeback in 1992 at the age of 40, trying to qualify for the Olympics in the butterfly. He needed a time of 55.59 to make the team but could only manage a 58.03. Here are how Spitz's 1972 marks compare with the current Olympic record:

Race	Current Record	Spitz's Time in 1972
200–meter butterfly	Michael Phelps 1:54.04	Spitz 2:00.70
100–meter butterfly	Michael Phelps 51.25	Spitz 54.27
100–meter freestyle	Pietr van den Hoogenband 47.84	Spitz 51.22
200–meter freestyle	Ian Thorpe 144.71	Spitz 1:52.78
4 x 200–meter freestyle relay	Australia 7:07.05	U.S. 7:35.78
4 x 100–meter medley relay	U.S. 3:30.68	U.S. 3:38.16
4 x 100–meter freestyle relay	South Africa 3:13.17	U.S. 3:38.84

The story goes that before the race Spitz told his coach Sherm Chavoor, "I think it would be better if I scratched myself from the 100-meter freestyle and saved myself for the 4 x 100 relay. Six gold medals isn't so bad."

Chavoor responded, "You mean five gold medals. If you don't swim the 100 meters, you're out of the relay. You might as well go home now. They'll say you're chicken, that you're afraid to face Jerry Heidenreich."

Spitz took up the challenge and in the semifinal heat finished third, behind Heidenreich and defending Olympic champion Michael Wenden of Austria. In the finals, Spitz rose to the occasion, nipping Heidenreich at the wall by four-tenths of a second. This was Spitz's closest victory of the Olympics, with a time of 51.22, slicing .25 seconds off his own world record.

The 4 x 100–medley relay: Spitz completed his record-setting seven-gold-medal performance as Michael Stamm, Tom Bruce, Heidenreich, and Spitz set another world record time of 3:48.16, topping the old mark of 3:50.4 held by Spitz and three other Americans.

With 11 career Olympic medals, Spitz (nine gold, one silver, and one bronze) tied the record held by marksman Carl Osburn (five gold, four silver, and two bronze) in shooting disciplines between 1912 and 1924. Swimmer Matt Biondi (eight, two, and one) would tie the record in 1996. Spitz didn't have much time to enjoy his triumph. Just hours after competing in his final race, Palestinian terrorists took hostage and eventually murdered 11 Israeli athletes in Munich Olympic Village. Spitz, who was Jewish, was quickly whisked away to London under heavy guard.

"I'D RATHER WIN SIX OUT OF SIX, OR EVEN FOUR OUT OF FOUR, THAN SIX OUT OF SEVEN. IT'S REACHED A POINT WHERE MY SELF-ESTEEM COMES INTO IT. I JUST DON'T WANT TO LOSE."
—MARK SPITZ

#32 DOUBLE OR NOTHING

EARL WEBB'S SINGLE-SEASON DOUBLES RECORD HAS BEEN STUBBORNLY RESISTANT

Boston right fielder Earl Webb, a rather ordinary player for all but one season of his career, laced 67 doubles in 1931—and never more than 30 in any other year. Photo courtesy of MLB Photos via Getty Images.

EVERY FEW YEARS, IN THE MIDDLE OF A baseball season, the press rediscovers Earl Webb. Usually by the All-Star break some player has 35 doubles or so.

Recently it was Todd Helton and Lyle Overbay. In seasons past it was John Valentin, Craig Biggio, Chuck Knoblauch, or John Olerud. In the Hall of Fame division, Wade Boggs and George Brett qualified. One of the best examples came in 1996, when reporters were predicting that Edgar Martinez wouldn't just break Webb's single-season record for doubles—67 set in 1931—but obliterate it. As of June 18 of that season, Martinez had 36 two-base hits and was on pace to hit 88. But what all these players learned was that "on pace" and "projected" don't get you into the record books. Martinez fell 15 doubles short of Webb that year, finishing with 52 doubles.

Just who is Earl Webb? A rather ordinary player who holds one of the most extraordinary records in Major League history. Webb, the right fielder for the Red Sox, started the 1931 season quickly and, as his total of two-baggers mounted, he was dubbed the "King of Dublin." He had 51 doubles by August 5, when the first controversy erupted: the Associated Press reported that his total had been revised to 50 because he had been credited accidentally, by an "unofficial scorer," with a double rather than a single

MAKE THAT FIVE DOUBLES

In 1970 Dal Maxvill of the St. Louis Cardinals hit only five doubles, setting a Major League record for the fewest doubles in a complete season (minimum 150 games played.) The fewest two baggers by a league leader is 28 by Heinie Groh of Cincinnati in 1918.

during a game on May 1. As his doubles total grew and he began threatening the record of 64, set by Cleveland's "Tioga George" Burns in 1926, people began to take notice. Webb set the record on his 37th birthday on September 17, 1931, hitting his 65th double against the Indians in the second game of a double-header in which the Sox would lose 2–1, a not-uncommon occurrence for a sixth-place team that lost 90 games.

The first thing that makes Webb's record truly amazing is that the right fielder never hit more than 30 doubles in any other season. In fact, he only reached double digits in doubles in four other seasons. Tris Speaker holds the career record with 792 doubles, while Webb had a career total of only 155.

The other strange thing is the record's surprising longevity. Webb's freshly minted record was challenged only a year later when Paul Waner of the Pittsburgh Pirates hit 62 doubles, the most all-time by a left-hander in the National League. In 1934, Hank Greenberg hit 63 doubles. In 1936, St. Louis's Joe

Medwick made a run at the record, hitting 64 doubles, the most all-time in the NL.

And yet Webb's record endures, although it's been under renewed attack. Between 2000 and 2006, five players—Helton, Carlos Delgado, Nomar Garciaparra, Garret Anderson, and Lance Berkman—have had at least 55 doubles.

Before 2000, when Helton hit 59 and Delgado hit 57, no player had hit more than 56 doubles since 1936.

"I don't know why that record has stood longer than the home-run record," said Astros first baseman Jeff Bagwell, who hit a career-high 48 doubles in 1996. "I would have thought someone would have hit 67 doubles before someone hit 70 home runs, but that's a tremendous amount of doubles."

Even this relatively obscure record is not without its controversy. At the time some suggested that late in the season Webb padded his total by occasionally slowing down on the base paths to turn a potential triple into a sure double. "I remember my father coming home from the game and saying, 'That dirty so-and-so, he stopped at second base again,'" recalled former Red Sox public relations director Bill Crowley.

In a 1996 *Sports Illustrated* article, Tim Kurkjian suggested that he was aided by a sloping embankment in left field known as Duffy's Cliff, although none of Webb's teammates, playing in the same park, hit more than 35 doubles.

How does Webb explain himself? After returning home, he told a Tennessee newspaper: "I've tried to figure that out but can't do it." Only two years after setting the record, Webb returned to the Tennessee coal mines. He died in 1965—at age 67.

Webb's career lasted just seven seasons in which he played for six teams. Bolstered by his career-high .333 average in 1931, he retired with a .306 lifetime average.

"I DON'T KNOW WHY THAT RECORD HAS STOOD
LONGER THAN THE HOME-RUN RECORD. I WOULD
        HAVE THOUGHT SOMEONE WOULD HAVE HIT 67
DOUBLES BEFORE SOMEONE HIT 70 HOME RUNS, BUT
THAT'S A TREMENDOUS AMOUNT OF DOUBLES."
                    —HOUSTON ASTROS STAR JEFF BAGWELL

TRIPLE OR NOTHING

While Earl Webb's single-season record for doubles has come under serious attack in recent seasons, the career record of 792 doubles by Hall of Fame outfielder Tris Speaker seems safe for the foreseeable future. The leader among players who played most of their careers during the post-1969 expansion era is George Brett with 665, while the active leader is Craig Biggio, who had collected 604 two-baggers by the end of the 2005 season.

Even more invulnerable is the record for triples. The career record is held by Hall of Famer Sam Crawford, who was safe at third a remarkable 309 times, 14 times more than second-place Ty Cobb. The active leader entering the 2006 season was Steve Finley with only 112.

The single-season triples mark seems equally unassailable. In 1912, John Owen "Chief" Wilson of the Pittsburgh Pirates hit an astonishing 36 triples. Wilson had never hit more than 13 doubles before he set the record and wouldn't top 14 afterward. And other than that gaudy triples total, Wilson's numbers that season looked rather average, with 80 runs scored, 95 RBIs, and a .300 average. Wilson had to contend with the huge outfield at Pittsburgh's Forbes Field—360 feet to left, 376 to right, and 462 feet to left center. Wilson hit 24 of his 36 three-baggers at home. His last triple came in the last game of the season, when he was thrown out at the plate trying for an inside-the-park grand slam. Only two players since 1950 have been able to hit more than 20 triples in a season—Willie Wilson of the Kansas City Royals and Lance Johnson of the New York Mets, who each hit 21 in 1985 and 1996, respectively.

GODDESS OF GOLD

SOVIET GYMNAST LARISSA LATYNINA WON MORE OLYMPIC MEDALS THAN ANY ATHLETE, MALE OR FEMALE

Soviet gymnast Larissa Latynina, owner of a record 18 medals through three consecutive Olympiads, competes in the women's compulsory exercises at the Tokyo Games in 1964. Photo courtesy of Getty Images.

HERE'S A TOUGHIE. WHICH ATHLETE HAS won more Olympic medals than any other? Give up? It's Soviet gymnast Larissa Latynina. Her record of 18 medals has endured for more than 40 years. Over the course of three consecutive Olympiads, she won nine gold medals, five silver, and four bronze.

Born in 1934 in Kherson, Ukraine, Latynina originally trained as a ballet dancer but switched to gymnastics after her choreography studio shut down. At the Olympics in Melbourne in 1956, at the age of 21, she began her record-breaking quest. She won six total medals, taking gold in the vault and the floor exercise, and winning both the team and the individual all-around competitions. She took silver in the uneven bars and bronze in the now-discontinued team competition with portable apparatus.

Four years later at the Rome Olympics Latynina again took home six medals, winning gold for the floor exercise, the team, and the all-around; silver for the uneven bars and balance beam; and bronze for the vault.

Latynina was 29 when she competed in her final Games, in Tokyo in 1964. As if out of habit, she again came home with six medals, winning gold in floor exercises and team competition; silver in the vault and the all-around; and bronze in uneven bars and balance beam.

MEDAL MADNESS

Between her Olympic efforts, Latynina earned 14 medals at the World Championships (nine gold, four silver, and one bronze), 14 medals at the European Championships (seven gold, six silver, and one bronze), and managed to find time to have three children.

Her nine gold medals set a women's record among athletes at the summer Olympics. The next closest is U.S. swimmer Jenny Thompson, who won eight gold medals competing in the 1992, 1996, and 2000 Games. Three men also have nine gold medals—Finnish runner Paavo Nurmi, swimmer Mark Spitz, and track star Carl Lewis.

Second all-time in total medals behind Latynina, and first among men, is gymnast Nikolai Andrianov of Russia, who won 15 medals, including six gold, at the 1972, 1976, and 1980 games. Czech gymnast Vera Caslavska is second to Latynina in total medals by a woman with 11 (seven gold, four silver) earned at the 1960, 1964 and 1968 games.

Between her Olympic efforts, Latynina earned 14 medals at the World Championships (nine gold, four silver, and one bronze), 14 medals at the European Championships (seven gold, six silver, and one bronze), and managed to find time to have three children. While women's gymnastics has become one of the marquee events of the Olympic Games, Latynina's accomplishments have largely been forgotten. In naming her the greatest gymnast of the period before 1970, *Inside Gymnastics* magazine wrote, "She didn't perform the most difficult routines nor the most innovative, but she imparted an especially classical, balletic style." But despite an unprecedented medal haul, Latynina couldn't even crack the top 10 of a readers' poll of the top female gymnasts of all time.

"SHE DIDN'T PERFORM THE MOST DIFFICULT ROUTINES NOR THE MOST INNOVATIVE, BUT SHE IMPARTED AN ESPECIALLY CLASSICAL, BALLETIC STYLE."

—*INSIDE GYMNASTICS* MAGAZINE

Latynina performs her routine on the beam in Melbourne, Australia, during the 1956 Games, where she won four gold medals. *Photo courtesy of AFP/Getty Images.*

#34 INTO THE RING

BILL RUSSELL AND HENRI RICHARD
WON MORE TITLES THAN ANY OTHER PLAYERS

Montreal Canadiens forward Henri Richard hugs the Stanley Cup after scoring the game-winning goal in overtime to defeat the Detroit Red Wings in the 1966 playoffs.

ONE IS CLOSE TO 7', THE OTHER IS NOT even 6'; they played different sports in different cities in different countries; and they don't even speak the same language, but Henri Richard of the Montreal Canadiens and Bill Russell of the Boston Celtics have one thing in common. They both have more championship rings—11—than they have fingers.

To put their championship dominance in some perspective, note that there are only two other *franchises*—the Yankees with 26 and the Lakers with 13—that have more titles than these two stars own individually. (The individual leaders in baseball and the NFL: Yogi Berra with 10 and Charles Haley, who won five Super Bowl rings with San Francisco and Dallas. Forrest Gregg won five championships with the Packers and one with the Cowboys for a total of six, three of them before the Super Bowl era.)

Before Russell arrived, the Celtics had never won a single title. In his first year, they changed that, and Russell made history, becoming the first player to win a title the year after taking the NCAA championship. The next year, the Celtics again advanced to the NBA finals, and Russell sprained his ankle in Game 3 against the Hawks. With the MVP sidelined, St. Louis won the championship in six games.

The next year, the Celtics began a run of eight straight titles that wouldn't end until the 1966–67

> "I WOULDN'T HAVE SAID IT BEFORE, BUT NOW THAT IT'S ALL OVER, I THOUGHT THAT WINNING LIKE THAT WAS NORMAL."
> —HENRI RICHARD

Russell (No. 6) and teammate Emmette Bryant run off the floor in Los Angeles after beating the Lakers again in 1969 for the Celtics' 11ᵗʰ championship in 13 years.

season, when Wilt Chamberlain's 76ers wrested the title away. The Celtics, with Russell as player-coach, came back and won back-to-back titles in 1967–68 and 1968–69. When he hung up his high tops the next year, Bill Russell had won 11 championships in only 13 years.

There are others with more NBA championship rings—notably Red Auerbach, who collected 16 rings, and K. C. Jones, who collected 12—but those included titles won while coaching or serving as GM. Russell played on every one of those 11 title teams.

"I played because I was dedicated to being the best," Russell explained. "I was part of a team, and I dedicated myself to making that team the best."

Henri Richard was perhaps not quite the dominant figure that Russell was, but his story was quite similar. The Canadiens won the Stanley Cup in his rookie year, the first of a record string of five consecutive championships. Henri was the much-younger brother of Montreal legend Maurice Richard, and because of his small stature, 5'7", 160 pounds, he was nicknamed the Pocket Rocket.

"I never thought I would wear the uniform of the Canadiens at the same time as my brother Maurice," Henri recalled. "Imagine, I was six years old when Maurice made his debut with the Canadiens, and I played five years with him."

TWICE AS NICE

If you combine Russell's and Richard's 11 championships apiece and come up with 22 between them, there is only one other *team* in the history of sports that has more titles: the New York Yankees with 26.

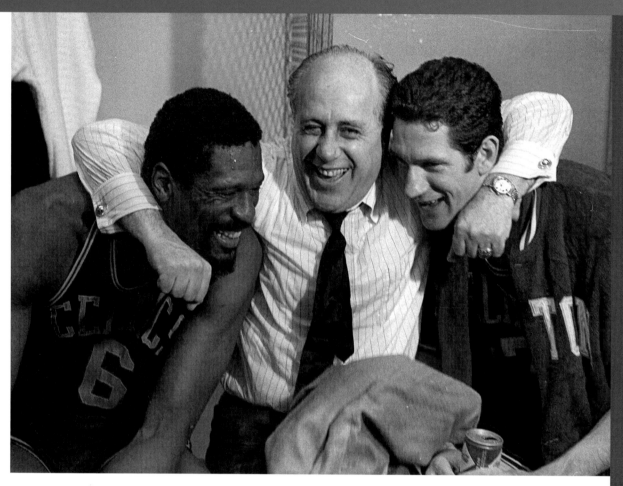

Coach Red Auerbach is flanked by two of his future Hall of Famers who helped him win the 1968 title—again— over the Lakers in Los Angeles: Russell and John Havlicek.

HENRI'S MISSING RINGS

In the loose way that sports-writers use the word ring interchangeably with title or championship, Henri Richard shares the record with Bill Russell. But any jeweler would tell you that Richard has one ring and one ring only. First off, only one ring was issued during that remarkable run of five titles in a row from 1956 to 1960. And then, all but one of Richard's remaining rings were stolen from his Laval home after his retirement. Richard received a phone call offering the return of the mementos in return for sub-stantial ransom, but none of them were ever recovered.

After a brief fallow period in the early 1960s, Montreal again rose to the top in the 1964–65 season and won the Stanley Cup four times in five years. Richard scored the Cup-winning goal in the 1966 Final against the Red Wings in overtime and netted the Cup clincher against Chicago in 1971. His 11th and last title came in 1972–73.

Some people say it was destiny, but Richard says, "I just think I was in the right place at the right time. That was a great team. There were so many great hockey players. I wouldn't have said it before, but now that it's all over, I thought that winning like that was normal."

#35 PASSING THE BOARDS

WHEN IT CAME TO REBOUNDING, WILT CHAMBERLAIN AND BILL RUSSELL WERE HEAD AND SHOULDERS ABOVE THE CROWD

Boston's Bill Russell (6) appears to have outreached Philadelphia's Wilt Chamberlain for this rebound during a 1967 game, but Wilt had the edge in career numbers. Chamberlain had 23,924 to Russell's 21,620, placing them (comfortably) at numbers one and two on the all-time list.

THE 20,000 REBOUND CLUB. IT MAY NOT have quite the ring of some other sports clubs, but its membership is oh-so-exclusive and likely to remain so for some time. Go to the NBA record book and you'll discover that Wilt Chamberlain holds the career record with 23,924 rebounds. Not far behind is Bill Russell, who has 21,620. The next closest is Moses Malone, well behind with 17,834.

Further research suggests that rebounding is something of a lost art in professional basketball. Wilt holds the seven best single-season rebounding marks, while Russell holds the next five on the list. Chamberlain is the only player in league history to grab 2,000 boards and owns the single-season record with 2,149 in 1961. Russell made a good run, grabbing 1,930 rebounds in 1964. Together, Chamberlain and Russell hold the top 18 single-season rebounding marks.

Only one player in the last 25 years has made the top 50 single-season rebounding list: Dennis Rodman. Nobody has cracked the top 25 since Wilt Chamberlain in 1972. And since 2000, only one player has managed to sneak into the top 100. In 2000, Dikembe Mutombo had 1,157 rebounds, the 95th best in history.

Chamberlain holds the single-season record for most rebounds per game with 27.20 in 1961, and six out of the top seven single-season records. Bill Russell's

Chamberlain gets the upper hand in grabbing a rebound over the Knicks' Walt Bellamy during a game in 1966.

best total was 24.74 in 1964, the fourth-highest ever. Together they hold the top 19 RPG seasons.

Chamberlain's peak was higher, but Russell sustained his greatness longer. Chamberlain also holds the edge in career rebounds per game, but the edge is slim: 22.89 to 22.45. The third highest is Bob Pettit, more than six rebounds per game below the two leaders with 16.22.

While the 7'1" Chamberlain would have been a big man in any era of basketball, Russell, at 6'9" and 220 pounds, would be an undersized power forward in today's game. So it's clearly not about physical superiority, it's about the pure desire to go out and grab the ball.

And of course, this rivalry was about more than mere stats. Rewind to November 24, 1960. That night Chamberlain had a game for the ages against the Celtics, setting the all-time record for rebounds in a single game with 55. (As you might expect, together Russell and Chamberlain hold the top 10 single-game marks, 46 of the top 50 single-game marks, and 85 of the top 100 single-game marks.) Chamberlain broke Russell's old record of 51 while holding his nemesis to a below-average 19 rebounds. Only one problem for Chamberlain: Russell's Celtics beat Chamberlain's Warriors 132–129.

CHAMBERLAIN HOLDS THE SEVEN BEST SINGLE-SEASON REBOUNDING MARKS, AND RUSSELL HOLDS THE NEXT FIVE ON THE LIST.

RODMAN'S RUN

Who holds the record for the most consecutive seasons leading the league in rebounding? It's not Wilt or Russell. That distinction belongs to Dennis Rodman, the 6'8" forward who won seven rebounding titles in a row between 1991–92 and 1997–98. During those years he played for three different teams (Detroit, San Antonio, and Chicago).

SHAQ'S SHORTCOMING

Just how impressive is 20,000 rebounds? Shaquille O'Neal is clearly the greatest center of his era and one of the greatest of all time. However, Shaq is number 28 on the career rebounding list with 10,541 rebounds. He has averaged around 750 rebounds a season the past three years. That means he would have to play 12 more seasons to reach 20,000 rebounds. That would make him 46 years old when he joined the club. Not very likely.

The only two members of the 20,000 career rebound club, Chamberlain (left) and Russell, share a laugh while recounting their amazing rivalry—one of the greatest individual rivalries in sports—during a tribute to Russell in Boston on May 26, 1999.

SPECIAL Ks

ROGER CLEMENS AND KERRY WOOD ARE BASEBALL'S SINGLE-GAME STRIKEOUT KINGS

"ONE, TWO, THREE STRIKES, AND YOU'RE out." The magic of that simple sequence evokes the classic song "Take Me Out to the Ball Game" and is echoed by those fans who tape Ks to the upper-deck façade. But when it came to making guys swing and miss, there were two pitchers who, on three special days, were better than anyone ever: Kerry Wood and Roger Clemens.

Entering the 1986 season, the question concerning Boston Red Sox right-hander Roger Clemens wasn't whether he would strike people out (as a rookie in 1984 he struck out nearly one batter per inning and notched 15 strikeouts in one start), it was whether he would be able to pitch at all. Shoulder problems had limited him to 15 starts the preceding season and had forced him to undergo arthroscopic surgery. So as he entered his April 29 start against the free-swinging Seattle Mariners with a 3–0 record, the team was cautiously optimistic that his arm troubles were behind him. By the end of the evening, Clemens had erased any doubts.

It was on a cold New England night in front of a crowd of 13,414 that Clemens and the Mariners—who would go on to shatter the major league record for strikeouts with 1,148—conspired to make history. He struck out the side in the first inning and didn't look back. He had nine strikeouts after four innings and fanned a record eight Mariners in a row through the middle innings. Entering the ninth, Clemens was on record pace with 18 strikeouts. He struck out his former University of Texas (and future Red Sox) teammate Spike Owen to lead off the ninth. That tied the nine-inning record of 19 that had been posted by the Providence Grays' Charlie Sweeney in 1884, and that had been tied by Tom Seaver, Steve Carlton, and Nolan Ryan. Clemens captured sole possession of the record one batter later by fanning Phil Bradley for the fourth time in the game. When Ken Phelps grounded out to end the game, it meant that there would be one single-game record that would elude Clemens that night. The single-game record for strikeouts still stands at 21 in a 16-inning effort by Tom Cheney of the Washington Senators on September 12, 1962.

Clemens fanned every batter in the Seattle lineup at least once, and caught eight of them looking. Perhaps most amazingly, Clemens did not walk a single batter.

By September 18, 1996, Roger Clemens had established himself as one of the great pitchers in baseball and one of the best in Red Sox history. The 1996 season was frustrating for Clemens (he had a 4–11 record on August 1) and many, including Red Sox GM Dan Duquette, thought that Clemens had reached the end of the line. Although he would leave for Toronto the next season, Clemens had something left in the tank,

Roger Clemens was simply masterful in his first 20-strikeout game against the Mariners on April 29, 1986.

as four subsequent Cy Young awards would prove. He started by fanning Ruben Sierra in the first, and he would strike out the side in the second, fifth, and sixth innings. He had 19 strikeouts entering the ninth, a fact which energized the tiny Detroit crowd of 8,779.

Catcher Bill Haselman was unaware of Clemens's record pace until a coach told him as he went out for the ninth. Haselman said, "I decided not to tell him he had 19, so he could go out there and concentrate on what we were trying to do."

Alan Trammell popped to first leading off, Ruben Sierra got a hit, and Tony Clark flied to left. Clemens's last chance was Travis Fryman, who ran the count to 2–2. "When I came up, I knew he had 19. I didn't know what the record was. I knew I didn't want to be the 20th," he recalled. "Truthfully, I was just trying to not strike out. I chased a forkball." Clemens too was oblivious to the fact that he had made history.

Then, 10 seasons later, the "Rocket" did it again, fanning 20 Detroit Tigers on September 18, 1996.

Haselman said, "I walked out to the mound and I said, 'You know what you just did, right?' He was all fired up and he goes, 'Yeah, we just tied Cy Young in wins,' or something like that. I said, 'You struck out 20.' He didn't know—he genuinely didn't know. It's incredible to think he had no idea he had just tied his own major league record."

Clemens threw 151 pitches, 101 for strikes. He surrendered four hits without walking a batter. This win also tied Cy Young for the franchise lead in victories with 192 and shutouts with 38.

On May 6, 1998, Kerry Wood was very much the National League reincarnation of the young Roger Clemens, a young, strapping, hard-throwing Texan, playing for a venerable franchise in a vintage jewel of a ballpark. And on this day, he wasn't facing the impatient Mariners or the hapless Tigers. Wood was penciled in to start against the division-leading Astros whose lineup featured such veteran stars as Craig Biggio, Derek Bell, Jeff Bagwell, and Moises Alou.

Wearing Nolan Ryan's No. 34 on his back, Wood started by striking out the side in the first, and repeated the feat in the fifth. He hit his stride in the seventh, fanning seven consecutive batters, and eight of nine. With 19 Ks already in the book—Wood had tied the NL record then shared by Steve Carlton, Tom Seaver, and David Cone—and the Wrigley crowd on their feet, the rookie right-hander faced Derek Bell. He blew him away with a nasty 1–2 breaking ball to capture the record.

Wood's 2–0 win qualifies as one of the most dominant pitching performances in history. The only player to get a hit off Wood was Ricky Gutierrez. His third-inning grounder, which deflected off of third baseman Kevin Orie's glove, could have been ruled an error. "He deserved it. I'll go up there and tell them to give me an error," said Orie, who stretched for the ball but didn't dive.

"I couldn't imagine ever doing this," Wood said after the win. "It's the greatest thrill anyone could be associated with. Roger is a great pitcher and he's definitely established himself." You can say that again.

FAN CLUB

In a nine-inning game, two pitchers have struck out 20 (Woods and Clemens), five pitchers have struck out 19 (Johnson, Cone, Ryan, Seaver, Carlton), and 10 pitchers have struck out 18 (Ben Sheets, Clemens, Randy Johnson in eight innings, Ramon Martinez, Bill Gullickson, Ron Guidry, Ryan, Don Wilson, Sandy Koufax, and Bob Feller). On May 8, 2001, Randy Johnson struck out 20 Reds in his nine innings of work, but isn't credited with tying Clemens and Woods because the game went 11 innings. Nolan Ryan struck out 19 batters on four different occasions, but only once in nine innings. The record for most strikeouts in nine by a minor league pitcher was set by Ron Necciai, who struck out 27 batters in a Class-D game between the Appalachian League Bristol Twins and the Welsh Miners on May 13, 1952. He allowed a ground ball out in the second, but recorded four strikeouts in the ninth after a batter reached on a strike-three passed ball.

#37 NIGHT AFTER NIGHT

THE LAKERS' 33-GAME WINNING STREAK
SET A STANDARD FOR ALL OF PRO SPORTS

NINE GAMES INTO THE LAKERS' 1971–72 season, future Hall of Famer Elgin Baylor retired. But as he stepped away from the game, the Lakers stepped up theirs.

The day after he retired, the Lakers began the longest winning streak in not only NBA history, but in American professional team sports: 33 games from November 5, 1971, to January 9, 1972. The streak began with a 110–106 victory over the Baltimore Bullets and ended after a 120–104 loss to the Milwaukee Bucks.

After starting the season 6–3, the Lakers won the final 14 games in November before going 16–0 in December and winning their first three games in January. That's more than two months without a loss. The Lakers won 17 at home and 16 on the road, and the streak included four trips to the East Coast.

The previous record winning streak was only 20, set by the Milwaukee Bucks the previous season. The best since then is the 19-game streak by the 1999–2000 Lakers.

On January 9, 1972, in Milwaukee, the Lakers streak finally came to an end. Los Angeles lost 120–104 to the defending NBA champion Milwaukee Bucks who, ironically, were led by future Lakers' legend Kareem Abdul-Jabbar. The Hall of Fame center had 39 points, 20 rebounds, 10 blocks, and five assists

Jerry West (left) of the Lakers and Philadelphia's Fred Carter race downcourt stride for stride during the Lakers' 154–132 win on December 19, 1971—their 25th consecutive win.

Wilt Chamberlain (left) sets a pick for teammate and future Hall of Famer West during the Lakers' 28th-straight win during the 1971–1972 season.

"ONCE THE STREAK STARTED ROLLING, IT WAS THE SNOWBALL EFFECT. YOU COULD
SEE THAT TEAMS DIDN'T THINK THEY COULD BEAT US. IT WAS LIKE MIKE
TYSON WHEN HE WAS BEATING EVERYBODY.
IT WAS JUST A MATTER OF WHICH PUNCH WAS GOING TO KNOCK YOU OUT."
—JIM MCMILLIAN

JUST WIN, BABY

The 1971–72 Lakers set not only an NBA record with their 33-game winning streak, they also set the standard for modern American professional sports. Here are the marks for each of the big four sports.

NBA: 1971–72 Lakers (33 games)   MLB: 1935 Chicago Cubs (21 games)

NFL: 2003–04 Patriots (21 games)   NHL: 1992–93 Penguins (17 games)

while outplaying Wilt Chamberlain (15 points, 12 rebounds, six blocks). The number Kareem wore? It was 33, of course.

Even with Baylor gone, the Lakers' lineup was loaded with Hall of Famers. Wilt Chamberlain was the center, and the backcourt featured Jerry West and leading scorer Gail Goodrich. "What's amazing about our streak, looking back, is that there was no need for last-second shots, no heroics like that," said Baylor's replacement, Jim McMillian. "There were games when we didn't play well, but we always found a way to win. Once the streak started rolling, it was the snowball effect. You could see that teams didn't think they could beat us. It was like Mike Tyson when he was beating everybody. It was just a matter of which punch was going to knock you out."

The Lakers finished that season with 69 wins, a single-season record that endured until Michael Jordan's Bulls broke it with 72 victories in the 1995–96 campaign. In winning the Pacific Division by 18 games, the Lakers also set records with 81 100-point games and a 63-point margin of victory against Golden State.

However, the streak would have meant little if the Lakers didn't take care of business in the playoffs. Since moving to L.A. from Minneapolis, the Lakers

had lost seven times in the finals—six times to the Boston Celtics—and most recently two years earlier against the Knicks.

In the Western Conference finals, the Lakers dethroned the Bucks in six games and got revenge over the Knicks in five games in the finals to give the franchise their first title in L.A. But while the Lakers lost the championship to the Knicks the following season, the legacy of the streak grows season by season.

"That will never be duplicated," predicted the late broadcaster Chick Hearn. So far, he's been right.

CONSISTENCY COUNTS

To put up 33 straight in the win column, a team is going to have to overcome some adversity. The 1971–72 Lakers didn't exactly get any breaks to put up their monster win streak—winning 17 of those games at home and 16 on the road. And to put today's media climate into perspective, where so much is made about East- and West-Coast road trips, the Lakers made a whopping four trips to the East Coast during the stretch.

#38 BYRON'S LORDSHIP

IN 1945 BYRON NELSON STRUNG
TOGETHER A MATCHLESS STREAK OF WINS

ELEVEN STRAIGHT WINS. THAT'S WHAT GOLF great Byron Nelson managed during his magical 1945 season. Unless, of course, he actually won a couple more.

At the beginning of the season, it didn't look like Nelson's year; his great rival Sam Snead started the year with four wins. Nelson's streak started in March at the Miami Four-Ball tournament at the Miami Springs Golf Course, a two-ball tournament where he was partnered with Jug McSpaden. He followed that up at the Charlotte Open where he beat Snead in a 36-hole playoff. He won three more tournaments—in Greensboro, Durham, and Atlanta—when the tour, deferring to wartime considerations, went on a two-month hiatus.

When the tour resumed, Nelson collected wins in Montreal, Philadelphia, and Chicago. He won the PGA championships at the Moraine Country Club in Ohio, the year's only major. Nelson followed that up with a win at the Tam O'Shanter in Chicago, where he topped Ben Hogan by 11 strokes. Nelson won the Canadian Open, and that, by official count, ended his streak.

Nelson's record has been under almost continuous attack, and no golfer has even gotten close. Tiger Woods and Ben Hogan are tied for second with six in a row.

Some golf experts, most notably Dan Jenkins, have argued that Nelson's streak was actually longer. In the middle of the run, during the tour's downtime, Nelson competed against Snead in a stroke-play event dubbed the World Championships, played over 72 holes at two courses: Fresh Meadows on Long Island and the Essex County Country Club in West Orange, New Jersey. Nelson won the event by four strokes, 272–276. After his Canadian Open win, Nelson won a 36-hole tournament in Spring Lake, New Jersey, where he beat Snead, among others. The purse was below the PGA minimum so it was not sanctioned by the tour.

"When the streak ended in Memphis a week later it was either 11, 12, or 13 in a row," wrote Jenkins.

However long it was, the record-breaking streak was just the highlight of the greatest season golf has ever seen. At one point, Byron recorded 22 straight rounds under par. Over those rounds, Nelson was a combined 83 under par. He never finished outside the top 10 of any tournament he played that year, and his worst score on a final round was a 71.

The year's other keystone accomplishment was Nelson's 18 total wins, also a record. To put this in perspective, only two other golfers have managed to

NELSON'S RECORD HAS BEEN UNDER ALMOST CONTINUOUS ATTACK,
AND NO GOLFER HAS EVEN GOTTEN CLOSE. TIGER WOODS AND
BEN HOGAN ARE TIED FOR SECOND WITH SIX IN A ROW.

A YEAR TO REMEMBER

Nelson's 11 straight victories in 1945 catapulted him to another remarkable record, 18 tour wins for the season. Never before and only three times since has another golfer reached double figures for wins in a season. Two of the best players to come along in the last 50 years, Tiger Woods and Vijay Singh, have each managed nine wins during incredible seasons of their own, exactly half that of Nelson's magical year of 1945.

Byron Nelson tees off at the All-American Golf Tournament in Chicago on July 28, 1945, in the midst of his amazing record of posting 11 straight wins.

Nelson (right) is awarded the PGA Championship trophy during his magical summer of 1945, in which he finished with 18 wins for the year, also a record.

break into double figures in wins in a season: Ben Hogan, who won 13 in 1946 and 10 in 1948, and Sam Snead, who won 13 in 1950. Among active golfers, the high-water mark is nine, held by Tiger Woods and Vijay Singh. And when he wasn't winning, Nelson was likely lurking; he finished second seven other times that year.

Entering that year, Nelson's resume was impressive. He won The Masters in 1937 and 1942, the U.S. Open in 1939, and the PGA Championship in 1940. In many ways the dominant 1945 season marked Nelson's swan song on the tour: he would play only one more year as a full-time touring pro.

As impressive as Nelson's record is, there are some mitigating factors. First is the fact that several of the events in which Nelson played in 1945 were two-man tournaments—a format that's fallen out of favor today. Also, the streak took place in the middle of World War II. The Masters and U.S. Open weren't played and fields were depleted, partly because many players— including Ben Hogan—were serving in the military, and partly because of travel restrictions that affected the remaining players.

Still, Nelson's record has stood the test of time, and the ever-increasing level of competition on the PGA Tour will only make it harder for a player to put together a streak of any length. "Under the current situation," said Nelson, "I don't believe anybody's going to do it."

#39

DEAN OF ATHLETICS

DEAN SMITH OF NORTH CAROLINA WON
MORE GAMES THAN ANY MEN'S DIVISION I COACH

Dean Smith shouts instructions to his players during a game in 1997. The North Carolina legend ended his career with a record 879 wins.

"REMEMBER, THEY HUNG ME IN EFFIGY in my early seasons with the Tar Heels," Dean Smith recalls. "Being hanged in effigy is fine, as long as they don't get me for real."

No, it wasn't always a picnic for college basketball's winningest coach, who faced down an angry mob of students in Chapel Hill after an early road loss to Wake Forest. But he got past that tough loss to amass more wins than any coach in the history of the game.

Smith's 879 wins is a remarkable achievement. Think about it this way. To break the record you'd have to win 25 games a year for 35 years—and then win five more games. (For the record, Smith won 25 or more a record 22 times, and 20 or more 27 years in a row.) To look at it another way, by the middle of the 2005–06 season, Phil Jackson hadn't yet passed Smith's win total, despite the NBA's 82-game schedule. Pro basketball legends Red Holzman and Chuck Daly retired well short of Smith's total.

It's a testament to the formidable nature of Adolph Rupp's old record of 876 wins that Smith clearly continued coaching until he reached the mark and retired almost immediately thereafter. But unlike some of his contemporaries, Smith wasn't obsessed with winning.

"If you make every game a life-and-death proposition, you're going to have problems," he counseled. "For one thing, you'll be dead a lot."

Along the way, Smith did far more than just win games. As a player, he learned the game from Phog Allen at Kansas (who learned it from James Naismith, the inventor of the game). When he took over at North Carolina, he came up with a wide variety of enduring innovations, from the foul-line huddle to the four-corners offense. Smith also recruited and coached a few decent players—Billy Cunningham, James Worthy, Vince Carter, Rasheed Wallace, Antawn Jamison, Jerry Stackhouse, Sam Perkins, and Kenny Smith. Oh, yes, and a skinny freshman guard named Michael Jordan. How does the old joke go? Who's the only one who could stop Michael Jordan? Dean Smith, who kept His Airness reined in enough that he only averaged 17.7 points per game.

Smith's success carried over into the NCAA tournament—to a point. His teams made the Big Dance a record 27 times, including a record streak of 23 in a row. Smith owns the record for tournament wins with 65, and his 11 trips to the Final Four are second only to John Wooden's of UCLA. That said, he only won two championships, which is surprising and perhaps the only flaw on his C.V.

The question about Smith's career win record, impressive as it is, is not whether it will be broken, but when and by whom. At the start of the 2005–06 season Bobby Knight, who coached at Texas Tech, Indiana

Smith is all smiles after this game on December 5, 1983, his 500th career win.

University, and Army, had 832 wins. If Knight gets the record, it's possible he won't hold it for long. Entering the 2005–06 season, Mike Krzyzewski, of Smith's archrival Duke, had 648 wins. At his current 25-wins-a-year pace, that puts the 58-year-old Coach K about nine and a half seasons away from Smith's mark. And then there's Harry Statham. In December 2004 the men's basketball coach at McKendree College, an NAIA school, won his 880th game with a win over Maryville. Smith may have been the first, but he probably won't be the last.

"IF YOU MAKE EVERY GAME A LIFE-AND-DEATH PROPOSITION,
YOU'RE GOING TO HAVE PROBLEMS. FOR ONE THING, YOU'LL BE DEAD A LOT."
—DEAN SMITH

Smith directs the Tar Heels during the Final Four in 1982, when North Carolina won the NCAA Tournament.

HEAD OF THE CLASS

Who's the winningest basketball coach in NCAA history? That would have to be Pat Head Summitt, who heads the women's program at the University of Tennessee. In March of 2005, she recorded her 880th win to pass Dean Smith. With the record-breaking win, Summitt improved her career record to 880–181, compared to Smith's 879–254. Amazingly, Summitt was only 52 years old when she reached the milestone, 14 years younger than Smith. When she began coaching at age 22, Summitt had to wash the team's uniforms and drive the van to road games. Overall, Summitt won six titles, including three in a row from 1996 to 1998, made 15 Final Four appearances, and won 87 tournament games, all eclipsing the equivalent men's coaching record.

On the women's side, Tennessee's Pat Summitt passed Smith's 879-game mark during the 2005–06 season.

#40

THE GRANDEST SLAMMER

ROD LAVER WON TENNIS'S BIGGEST PRIZE—
NOT ONCE, BUT TWICE

TENNIS'S GRAND SLAM TOURNAMENTS are downright Darwinian. To win, you must get through seven best-of-five-set matches. Unlike, say, the football or baseball playoffs, where you can lose games and still have a chance to become champion, this is single-elimination: one misstep, one off day, one bad break, and you're sent packing. Survival of the fittest.

No wonder that only five players in tennis's 100-year-plus history have won all four majors in singles in a calendar year, a rare accomplishment called the Grand Slam. But only one player has been able to pull off the sport's greatest feat twice: the redheaded left-hander from Australia, Rod Laver.

No one saw it coming. As a child growing up in Queensland, Australia, Laver was a scrawny and often sickly kid. When he was a teenager, Australian Davis Cup captain Harry Hopman sarcastically nicknamed him "Rocket." But Laver was tougher than he looked and turned his 5'8", 150-pound frame into a brutally efficient winning machine.

"He was anything but a Rocket," Hopman once said. "But Rod was willing to work harder than the rest, and it was soon apparent to me that he had more talent than any other of our fine Australian players."

In 1962, as an amateur, Laver captured his first Grand Slam, winning the Australian championships, French Open, Wimbledon, and the U.S. championships. Do the math: that's 28 consecutive matches over the course of a year. Laver, who sported a mammoth Popeye left forearm with which he generated fierce topspin, was dominant.

After finishing the year number one and helping Australia win a fourth Davis Cup, Laver turned pro. This was a big move because, according to tennis's arcane rules at that time, professionals were barred from Grand Slam tournaments. For most of the 1960s, Laver passed on a chance to burnish his record in favor of earning a living. But in 1968, tennis began its so-called Open Era, allowing pros to enter the Grand Slams—and Laver was back in action. A year later, Laver amazingly won the Grand Slam again, and this time against much stiffer competition.

How tough a task is the Grand Slam? Aside from Laver, only one player in the Open Era—American Andre Agassi—has been able to win all four Grand Slam tournaments in a career. But Laver's legacy is largely one of what might have been. What if Laver had remained an amateur throughout the 1960s and contested all those lost Slams? Three Slams? Four? Sadly, we'll never know.

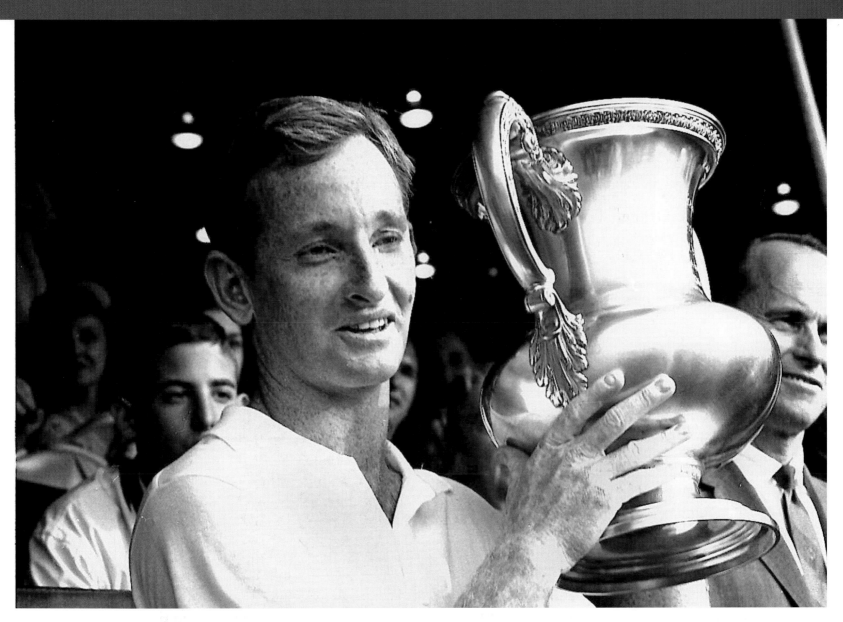

Australian amateur Rod Laver hoists the National Tennis Championships (now the U.S. Open) trophy at Forest Hills, New York, during his first Grand Slam summer of 1962.

"ROD WAS WILLING TO WORK HARDER THAN THE REST, AND IT WAS SOON APPARENT TO ME
THAT HE HAD MORE TALENT THAN ANY OTHER OF OUR FINE AUSTRALIAN PLAYERS."
—AUSTRALIAN DAVIS CUP CAPTAIN HARRY HOPMAN

Laver returns a backhand during his quarterfinal match in the 1969 French Open at Roland Garros Stadium in Paris.

THE OTHER SLAMMERS

The only other man to win a grand slam was Don Budge in 1938, but three women accomplished the feat:

Maureen Connally	1953
Margaret Court	1970
Steffi Graf	1988

Three doubles teams also completed the Grand Slam:

Frank Sedgman and Ken McGregor	1951
Margaret Smith and Ken Fletcher	1963
Martina Navratilova and Pam Shriver	1984

The players who completed a career grand slam in singles are:

Fred Perry
Doris Hart
Shirley Fry
Roy Emerson
Billie Jean King
Chris Evert
Andre Agassi

Two other men managed to win a slam on every surface. While Jimmy Connors never won the French Open, he did win the 1976 U.S. Open when it was played on clay. And Mats Wilander of Sweden never triumphed at Wimbledon, but he managed to win the Australian Open when it was contested on grass.

ROGER THIS

By winning three of the four Grand Slam events in 2004—the Australian, Wimbledon, and the U.S. Open—Roger Federer has tennis fans thinking "slam." And while Federer is supremely gifted, with a classic all-court game that's a bit reminiscent of Laver's, he faces a hurdle that Laver didn't encounter—the Slams are now played on four distinct surfaces: Rebound Ace (a neutral, rubbery surface) at the Australian, slow red clay at the French, slick grass at Wimbledon, and a fast, hard court at the U.S. Open. In Laver's day, three of the four majors were contested on grass, with only Roland Garros on clay. Even if Federer can become the first man since Laver to win the Grand Slam, it's highly unlikely the 25-year-old will do it twice. And there is no chance whatsoever that he can break the record with three slams.

#41 TOUR DE FORCE

LANCE ARMSTRONG DEFEATED MORE THAN HIS RIVAL RIDERS TO WIN A RECORD SEVEN TOURS DE FRANCE

American cyclist Lance Armstrong celebrates winning the ninth stage of the 1999 Tour de France, which he would ultimately win as his first of an astounding seven straight Tour victories.

THE MOST AMAZING PART OF THE LANCE Armstrong story is, of course, the fact that he survived to compete in the Tour de France at all. The story is familiar, but it bears retelling.

A promising young rider with a World Championship under his belt, Armstrong put in a disappointing performance at the 1996 Olympics. Only weeks later he found out that he had testicular cancer. The cancer metastasized to his brain and lungs and doctors actually lied to Armstrong about his 10 percent chance of survival. Even faced with grim odds, Armstrong chose treatment options that would at least give him a chance of returning to race.

Armstrong not only survived, he came back to race as a changed rider. Before his illness, Armstrong's Tour de France results were far from spectacular—he dropped out three times, and finished 36th the only time he was able to make it to Paris. But after his treatments, Armstrong dropped 15 pounds and his improved power-to-weight ratio suddenly made him a formidable climber on the Tour's crucial mountain stages. In his return to the Tour de France in 1999, he won the opening prologue time trial and went on to win the race. It was an inspirational story, to be sure, but skeptics remained unconvinced, noting that such top contenders as Jan Ulrich and Marco Pantani were absent from the 1999 edition.

Armstrong, leading the pack (yellow jersey) up Tamie Pass between the French and Italian Alps, transformed himself into a dominant force on the mountain stages of the race.

Armstrong silenced those critics the next year with a dominating victory, riding away from his opponents on the treacherously steep Hautacam climb in one of cycling's great moments.

And from there, he just kept right on dominating, with convincing wins in the 2001 and 2002 Tours to run his string to four. The 2003 Tour was Armstrong's first date with destiny, as he successfully attempted to tie the record for tour wins held by Jacques Anquetil, Eddy Merckx, Bernard Hinault, and Miguel Indurain—this last of whom was the only other rider to win his five Tours in succession. Armstrong crossed that hurdle only to fly again in the face of history. All four of the other five-time Tour winners faltered quite suddenly and spectacularly in their quest for a sixth. Would Armstrong do the same?

Despite a rather undramatic race, it soon became evident he would not. As his rivals self-destructed one by one, Armstrong rode a rather conservative race and

ROUGE, BLANC ET BLU

While Lance Armstrong is the greatest American Tour rider, he's not the first. That honor went to Greg LeMond, who won the race in 1986 after finishing third and second in his first two Tours. LeMond was shot by his brother-in-law in a hunting accident two months before the 1987 Tour and didn't compete again until 1989. That year LeMond made a remarkable comeback, taking the yellow jersey away from race-leader Fignon on the final time trial into Paris, his margin of eight seconds the narrowest in Tour de France history. He won his third Tour the following year.

Armstrong again leading the pack during the late stages of his first Tour victory in 1999.

A MATTER OF LIFE OR DEATH

Armstrong's heroic Tour de France career as a cancer survivor seems to have enabled him to cheat death. However, others have not been so lucky. Three riders have been killed while riding in the race. In 1935 Francisco Cepeda died after falling down a ravine near the Col du Galibier. In 1967, Tommy Simpson died of heart failure on Mount Ventoux, possibly as a result of amphetamine abuse. And the most recent fatality hit Armstrong close to home. In 1995, his teammate Fabio Casartelli died after a crash while descending the Col de Portet d'Aspet. Three days after the accident Armstrong won a stage and pointed to the sky in tribute to his fallen friend. In 2001, Armstrong again honored Casartelli with a stage win, when the race again passed the site of the accident. "It's good to win, but the most special thing for me was thinking about Fabio," he said. "I won for him."

put his name in the record books all alone. There was some speculation that with the record safely his, Armstrong would retire at age 33, a ripe old age for a world-class cyclist. Instead, driven in part by commercial considerations—the Discovery Channel replaced the U.S. Postal Service as the title sponsor of the team—Armstrong decided to return for one more round.

On the one hand, Armstrong's dominance in the event is remarkable in that a mere moment of weakness, a falter on a mountain pass, a fall in a time trial, or even something as simple as a common cold or a saddle boil can sabotage a Tour bid. On the other hand, the Tour is definitely a race of streaks. So while Armstrong's record seems unassailable, Indurain's five in a row seemed equally unbreakable until Armstrong's miracle comeback.

ARMSTRONG NOT ONLY SURVIVED, HE CAME BACK TO RACE AS A CHANGED RIDER.
AFTER HIS TREATMENTS, ARMSTRONG DROPPED 15 POUNDS AND HIS
IMPROVED POWER-TO-WEIGHT RATIO SUDDENLY MADE HIM A FORMIDABLE CLIMBER
ON THE TOUR'S CRUCIAL MOUNTAIN STAGES.

42

GIVEN THE BOOT

HAVING ONLY HALF A FOOT DIDN'T STOP TOM DEMPSEY FROM KICKING THE LONGEST FIELD GOAL EVER IN THE NFL

Jason Elam of the Broncos celebrates his own 63-yarder at Mile High Stadium in Denver, tying the record 28 years after Dempsey's kick.

IT JUST MIGHT BE THE ULTIMATE BACKHANDED compliment for an athlete—when they rewrite the rule book because of you. But unlike towering college basketball centers Lew Alcindor and Bob Kurland, New Orleans Saints kicker Tom Dempsey was hardly an imposing physical specimen.

Born with half a right foot and no right hand, Dempsey wore a modified shoe with a flattened and enlarged toe area that looked a little like a hammer. Despite his awkward appearance—Dempsey had a huge belly in addition to his deformities—he generated tremendous power and distance, using a straight-ahead style that's a marked contrast to today's soccer-style kickers.

Never was that distance more apparent than on November 8, 1970, when the Saints hosted the Detroit Lions in Tulane Stadium. During the week prior to the game, New Orleans, which had won only one game all year, had fired head coach Tom Fears and replaced him with J. D. Roberts. Then, as now, firing a football coach in midseason was considered unusual and the Saints came up with an inspired effort for their new leader.

Still, given their expansion-team talent, that effort merely kept the game close and the Saints found themselves trailing 17–16 in the final seconds. New Orleans had not even reached midfield, but they

brought in the kicking team, because in those days the goalposts sat right on the goal line, making any field goal attempt 10 yards closer than it would be today. The line of scrimmage was the Saints' 45-yard line, which meant that Dempsey would kick the ball from the New Orleans 37 in an attempt to win the game. He had made many kicks from beyond that distance in practice and he felt confident as he came in to attempt the kick.

"The distance didn't scare me," Dempsey recalled years later. "I knew I had to hit it with everything I had. I felt that if I did that and all the other circumstances went well, I had a good chance of making that kick."

The other circumstances included the snap of center Jackie Burkett and the hold of Joe Scarpati. Old game films show that they were perfect, as was Dempsey's kick. "I thought I kicked it pretty well—I thought it had a chance," Dempsey said. "I was hoping the winds wouldn't swirl and drive the ball off-course. It seemed like it took forever to get there. I just kept watching it, wondering if it had enough distance. Finally, the referees raised their hands that it was good."

The ball barely made it over the goalposts on the game's final play and it gave the Saints a 19–17 win in a game that was memorable only because of that field goal.

The kick broke the record for the NFL's longest field goal, held at the time by Baltimore's Bert

The Saints' Tom Dempsey, with a custom-made shoe to fit his foot, kicks a record-setting, game-winning 63-yard field goal on November 8, 1970.

THE 60–AND–OVER CLUB

Only two other kickers besides Tom Dempsey and Jason Elam have managed to kick one from 60 yards or more in a regular-season game. Steve Cox of the Browns made a 60-yarder against Cincinnati on on October 21, 1984, and Morten Andersen of the Saints matched that feat against Chicago on October 27, 1991. Andersen also owns the NFL record for the most 50 yarders (40) in a career.

Rechichar, who connected on a 56-yarder in 1953. Rechichar lasted 10 years in the NFL as a defensive back and place-kicker.

When Dempsey's career came to an end following the 1979 season, the NFL decided that kickers could no longer wear "special" shoes, and that all equipment had to be "normal." Just call it the Tom Dempsey rule.

Tom Dempsey's name stood alone in the NFL record books until 1998, when Bronco place-kicker Jason Elam matched his mark with a 63-yarder of his own against Jacksonville in the thin air of Mile High Stadium on October 25. While Dempsey's kick was a game-winner with no time left on the clock, Elam's came at the end of the first half.

Elam's field-goal attempt was originally supposed to be a 58-yarder, but the Broncos were penalized for delay of game and that pushed the ball back five yards.

After the game, Elam was asked why he didn't have holder Tom Rouen move back an extra yard so he would have the record to himself. "Well, that gets kind of scary when you do that," Elam explained. "Everything is so precise with the snapper and holder. My snapper (David Diaz-Infante) is usually so good that he can snap to where holder Tom (Rouen) doesn't even have to move the laces at all. I never like to mess with that."

After Elam made his kick, Dempsey sent the Broncos kicker a congratulatory note the next day and Elam subsequently called Dempsey as they both relived their glory.

"I admired him because I knew what it took," Dempsey said. "I faxed him a letter the next day, and he called me back and we talked for a while.

"I wanted to congratulate Jason because when I set the record, Bert Rechichar was very gracious to me. He called to congratulate me, sent me a telegram. I told Jason that if someone breaks our record, it would be up to him to do the same thing. He just laughed."

"THE DISTANCE DIDN'T SCARE ME. I KNEW I HAD TO HIT IT
WITH EVERYTHING I HAD. I FELT THAT IF I DID THAT AND
ALL THE OTHER CIRCUMSTANCES WENT WELL, I HAD A GOOD
CHANCE OF MAKING THAT KICK."
—TOM DEMPSEY

CAMPUS KICKERS

While the level of play in the NFL may be much higher than in college football, the goalposts are the same, so collegiate kicking records take on a special significance. The longest field goal in Division I-A play was 67 yards, a feat accomplished by three players. Russell Erxleben of Texas did it against Rice on October 1, 1977. Steve Little of Arkansas matched the feat two weeks later against Erxleben's Texas squad. And a year later, Joe Williams of Wichita State tied the record versus Southern Illinois on October 21, 1978. All three kickers had the advantage of kicking off a then-legal 2" tee. Using the same type of tee, Ove Johansson of Abilene Christian, an NAIA school, kicked a 69-yarder against East Texas State on October 16, 1976—a kick considered by many to be the unofficial world record.

The longest Division I-A field goal kicked under current snap-and-hold rules was a 65-yarder by Martin Gramatica of Kansas State against Northern Illinois in 1998. He reportedly once kicked a 77-yarder in a collegiate practice game.

The Canadian Football League field-goal record is 63 yards, achieved by Paul McCallum in 2001.

Ola Kimrin kicked a 65-yard field goal in a preseason game against the Seattle Seahawks in Denver on August 29, 2002. However, because Kimrin was playing for the Broncos, where record-holder Jason Elam was the incumbent, he was cut shortly after making the kick.

#43

HIT PARADE

NO MAJOR LEAGUER TOPPED 250 HITS FOR 80 YEARS— UNTIL ICHIRO CAME ALONG

Seattle's Ichiro Suzuki tips his cap during a ceremony in honor of his breaking George Sisler's 84-year-old single-season-hits record in 2004.

THERE HAVE BEEN MANY INSTANCES IN which a Japanese player broke a Major League Baseball record—Sadaharu Oh broke Hank Aaron's home-run record, Sachio Kinugasa broke Lou Gehrig's consecutive-games streak before Cal Ripken did, and Yutaka Fukumoto topped Lou Brock in career steals before Rickey Henderson topped him. But all of these were done in Japanese baseball.

On October 1, 2004, Ichiro Suzuki, playing for the Seattle Mariners, broke one of Major League Baseball's most venerable records, the single-season-hits mark set by George Sisler of the St. Louis Browns in 1920. So when Suzuki singled in the third inning for his record-breaking 258th hit of the year, history was made in more ways than one.

ICHIRO'S SLOW START

Ichiro was the first Japanese position player to sign with a Major League club. He began his career with the Orix BlueWave. He clashed with his first manager over his unconventional batting style, and despite flashes of brilliance—notably a homer against Hideo Nomo—Suzuki spent most of his first two years on the farm team. When he was given a chance by a new manager, Ichiro responded by setting a Japanese single-season record with a then–Pacific League record 210 hits in 130 games. He also hit .385 and won the first of a record seven-consecutive batting titles.

Suzuki tied the record in the first inning after hitting a single on an 0–2 count and added another hit to finish the game 3–for–5. Five members of the Sisler family joined the 45,473 in attendance at sold-out Safeco Field to witness the record being broken. Suzuki was the first serious challenger to Sisler's record in more than 70 years, when Bill Terry of the New York Giants had 254 hits in 1930. Of the top 10 all-time single-season-hits leaders, Suzuki is the only player who did it after 1930.

While Sisler was elected to the Hall of Fame, his career is largely one marked by what might have been. "He missed the entire 1923 season with 'poisonous sinusitis' that caused double vision, and though Sisler returned to the field in 1924 and played seven more seasons, he was never the same player," suggested ESPN's Rob Neyer. "If Sisler's career had progressed naturally from that point, today he would be remembered as one of the greatest hitters ever."

Right-hander Ryan Drese was the Rangers pitcher who gave up the record-breaking hit, but he seemed not to grasp its historical impact. "It's not like it's the 500th home run or something like that. It's just a little single on the ground. It's no big deal."

Some critics dwelled on the fact that most of Suzuki's hits were singles; with 225 he shattered Wee Willie Keeler's mark of 206 set in 1898.

Matt Stairs of the Royals argued that Suzuki actually faced tougher conditions than Sisler. "The thing nowadays is it's a lot harder than it was 80 years ago because you've got specialty guys in the bullpen who have adjusted to his unique style of hitting. I've heard the comment by people that it's mostly singles. Well, I don't care." Indeed, the AL average in 2004 was .268, while in 1920 it was .283. And AL managers seemed to side with Stairs instead of Drese; Suzuki led the American League with 19 intentional walks, ahead of sluggers like Manny Ramirez.

Suzuki finished the year with a .372 batting average, 262 hits, 24 doubles, five triples, 49 walks, and 63 strikeouts, and he challenged the record books on a few other fronts. The former Orix BlueWave player ended the season with 924 hits in his four-year major league career, setting a new record for hits over any four-year span. The previous record was 918, set by Bill Terry from 1929 to 1932. Sisler was the only other player besides Suzuki and Terry to record more than 900 hits over four consecutive seasons, with 913 hits from 1920 to 1924. And batting leadoff he registered 704 at-bats, falling just one short of the ML record of 705, set by Willie Wilson in 1980. And perhaps his most intriguing accomplishment was buried in the stat splits—in 2004, Suzuki hit .429 after the All-Star break.

"I'm not a big guy and hopefully kids could look at me and see that I'm not muscular and not physically imposing, that I'm just a regular guy," said baseball's all-time single-season-hits king. "So if somebody with a regular body can get into the record books, kids can look at that. That would make me happy."

Ichiro raps a single back up the middle, his 255th hit of the season in pursuit of the record, against the Oakland A's on September 29, 2004.

50/50 PROPOSITION

In 2004, Ichiro also collected 50 hits in three different months and became the first player since Joe Medwick in 1936 to have back-to-back 50-hit months. "The 50 hits I got in May and the 50 hits I got in July and August are completely different," Suzuki explained. "You have an expression here when someone's going good that he's 'in the zone.' Basically, I don't believe in that because it means you attribute your success to some indefinable phenomena, but if that ever applied to me, last May might be a decent example. I wasn't entirely sure why I was getting all those hits because I actually felt like I wasn't consistently hitting pitches I expected to.

"But that wasn't the case in July and August. Through trial and error, I had discovered something meaningful that allowed me to get those hits. In virtually every case, I could clearly explain to you why I was able to hit each pitch. The number may have been the same each month—50—but the reason for the results was entirely different."

"I'M NOT A BIG GUY AND HOPEFULLY KIDS COULD LOOK AT ME AND SEE THAT I'M NOT MUSCULAR AND NOT PHYSICALLY IMPOSING, THAT I'M JUST A REGULAR GUY."
—ICHIRO SUZUKI

44

BIGGEST MAN ON CAMPUS

THREE COACHES DESERVE CONSIDERATION FOR THE COLLEGE COACHING WIN RECORD

Florida State coach Bobby Bowden, the winningest coach in college football, watches his team prepare for the 2005 season, his 30th at the helm.

GRIDIRON, GRIDIRON ON THE FIELD...
To which college coach must all others yield? That depends on how you look at the question.

Number one on the all-time list is Eddie Robinson at Grambling, who notched a record 408 wins.

He put that small and predominantly black college on the map, turning it into a mini-powerhouse, with four of his former players—Willie Brown, Willie Davis, Buck Buchanan, and Charlie Joiner—going on to merit induction into the Pro Football Hall of Fame. In total, 21 Grambling players have played in the Super Bowl, including Doug Williams, who became the first African American quarterback to win the NFL championship. Robinson also holds the record for most games coached (588) and longest football coaching career at one school (56 years). That said, Grambling isn't a Division I-A school.

The major college record belongs to Florida State's Bobby Bowden. He earned that distinction as the winningest coach in major college history in 2003, with 359 wins as of the beginning of the 2006 season. Bowden led his team to an astonishing 14 straight seasons in the Associated Press season-ending top five. He's coached two national championship teams, including the 1999 squad that was the first ever to go through a season from start to finish as the AP number one.

"I guess I've done okay," said the self-deprecating Bowden. "I'm just trying not to screw up. The great coaches of the game all become legends."

Bowden is neck-and-neck with another active legend, Joe Paterno of Penn State. Paterno, who has 354 career victories as head coach of the Nittany Lions, held the record briefly before being passed by Bowden. Indeed, many Paterno supporters argue that 31 of Bowden's wins should not be counted, as they came while Bowden was the head coach at Howard College, which is now Samford University, a Division I-AA football program. Bowden is credited with the record because the NCAA rule states that to be eligible for the record, a coach needs 10 years at a Division I-A school, at which point any and all wins at a four-year school are counted toward the career total.

WHO'S THE ONE?

Supporters of Joe Paterno argue that Bobby Bowden's 31 victories at Howard College—now Samford University—should be discounted as Division I-AA contests, but the NCAA rules support Bowden. Despite the apparent controversy, the two coaching legends remain close friends.

Bowden gets a shower from team members after the Seminoles defeated Virginia Tech 46–29 in the Sugar Bowl on January 4, 2000, securing a perfect 12–0 season and the national championship.

"I GUESS I'VE DONE OKAY. I'M JUST TRYING NOT TO SCREW UP.
THE GREAT COACHES OF THE GAME ALL BECOME LEGENDS."
—BOBBY BOWDEN

Wearing his trademark white socks, Paterno began his coaching career before the Eisenhower Administration; he has won games in six different decades. Paterno's 21 wins in bowl games give him the all-time lead among Division I-A coaches while Bowden is close behind with 19. Despite the closeness of the competition and the frequent comparisons between the two, Paterno and Bowden are actually close and longtime friends.

Both Bowden and Paterno passed the legendary Alabama coach Paul "Bear" Bryant, who ended his career with a 323–85–17 record and six national championships—1961, 1964, 1965, 1973, 1978, and 1979. His Alabama teams played in a bowl 24 straight years. In November of 1981, the Crimson Tide beat Auburn 28–17 to give Bryant his 315th win, which pushed him past Amos Alonzo Stagg, who set the record while coaching for Springfield College, the University of Chicago, and the College of the Pacific. On December 29, 1982, Alabama beat Illinois 21–15 in Bryant's last game as head coach. He died less than a month later in Tuscaloosa.

"I'm not much of a golfer, I don't have any friends, and all I like to do is go home and be alone and worry about ways not to lose," Bryant said, reflecting the single-mindedness necessary to win college football games by the hundreds.

Penn State head football coach Joe Paterno pauses during a news conference following a 2003 game against Ohio State.

NEW SCHOOL, OLD SCHOOL

Nearing his 80th birthday, and having strung together four losing seasons, Joe Paterno was beginning to hear whispers that the game had passed him by. "Act like you expect to get into the end zone," he would tell his players.

Before the 2005 season, the Penn State legend dispatched a number of his assistants to Texas to learn the spread offense from Texas coach Mack Brown. During the season, Paterno revamped his offense entirely, employing state-of-the-art three- and four-receiver sets as part of a wide-open post-millennium passing attack. The result? An 11–1 record, and the Nittany Lions came within one play of giving Paterno his sixth undefeated season. Who says you can't teach an old coach new tricks?

45

THE LONGEST YARDS

A 64-YEAR-OLD TEACHING PRO HIT THE LONGEST DRIVE IN GOLF HISTORY

Mike Austin was a 64-year-old teaching pro when he hit his record-setting shot at the U.S. National Seniors Open Championship in Las Vegas.

THE APPEAL OF GOLF FOR MANY IS THAT on any given shot almost anything can happen. A hole in one. A 50-foot birdie putt from off the green. Or just whacking the ball a quarter of a mile.

So exactly what is the record for longest drive? It's not the 412-yard monster that Tiger Woods hit in a practice round at the British Open in 1998. It's not even the 448-yard blast by Rory Sabbatini. If you ask the PGA, they'll tell you that Davis Love III hit it. At the Mercedes Championships in 2004, Love smashed a 476-yard drive, surpassing that of the previous record holder, Chris Smith, who held the record at 427 yards. Granted Love had a tailwind and the hole played downhill, but a 476-yard drive is a 476-yard drive.

And there are, of course, those long driving competitions. Jason Zuback cracked a ball 412 yards, and Sean "the Beast" Fister won the RE/MAX Long Drive Championship last year with a 377-yard shot. But there's one shot that tops them all. And that belongs to Mike Austin.

"It was like God held the ball in the air." That's how Tonya Austin recalled the 515-yard drive that her husband, Mike Austin, hit in the U.S. National Seniors Open Championship in Las Vegas in 1974. On this seemingly impossible drive, the then-64-year-old Austin had a 27-miles-per-hour tailwind at his back and perhaps a little help from the man upstairs. The

ball sailed clear of the green, 450 yards away, and was measured at an astonishing 515 yards, the longest recorded shot in a professional golf tournament.

Austin recalled the moment of his miracle shot: he had told the group ahead of them to stand clear. He then took out his Wilson Persimmon-headed driver with a 10-degree loft and an extra-stiff 43" steel shaft.

"I knew I knocked the hell out of it," Austin said. "But the ball went up strangely. Went out about 10 or 15 feet high and kept going and going at that flattened level. I could put my finger on it the whole way before it dropped."

Chandler Harper was one of the men playing in Austin's group that day.

"I had never seen a ball hit anywhere near that far. I played 50 times with Sam Snead and Ben Hogan, but nothing compared to this."

Was this a minor miracle? Austin would have politely disagreed. Hitting a golf ball gargantuan distances was Austin's specialty. He had a unique gift for hitting the golf ball incredible distances and claims to have hit a 400-yard drive as early as 1937. How is it possible that the longest hitters on tour have never even come close to Austin's mark?

Maybe it was all in his head. Austin, you see, studied physics and engineering at Emory University and earned a Ph.D. in kinesiology, the science of

Tiger Woods blasted a 412-yard monster drive during a practice round before the 1998 British Open—and still came up more than 100 yards short of Austin's unbelievable feat.

human movement. This scientific approach to the golf swing allowed him to create a revolutionary swing that could yield incredible amounts of power. Art Sellinger, two-time national long drive champion and cofounder of Long Drivers of America, said, "This guy had a swing that was 40 years ahead of his time. Mike Austin could get more out of less than anyone."

Why isn't Mike Austin a household name? Because his short game was as weak as his drives were strong. He played briefly on the PGA Tour, but his best finish came in the 1961 Ontario Open, where he tied for 37th place.

In fact, after Austin launched his historic 515-yard drive, he proceeded to pitch back onto the green and three-putt. Austin hit the longest drive in the history of golf, and he ended up making bogey.

As they say: "Drive for show, putt for dough."

IT'S A LONG DRIVE . . .

Babe Ruth hit a blast out of Sportsman's Park in 1915 that traveled an estimated 470 feet. In Detroit in 1926 he hit one that probably traveled 500 feet. Mickey Mantle is credited with two monumental blasts: a 1953 homer at Griffith Stadium that is said to have traveled 565 feet and a 634-foot round-tripper at Briggs Stadium in 1960 that landed him in the *Guinness World Records* book. However the measurements for both homers are questionable. The longest home run measured during Major League Baseball's *Tale of the Tape* program was Cecil Fielder's 502-foot blast in Milwaukee in 1991.

LABORATORY TESTS SHOW

Skeptics wondered how anyone, let alone a 64-year-old teaching pro, could hit a 515-yard drive. So they took it to the lab to find out. Given the 88-degree temperatures, the 27-miles-per-hour tailwind, and the 2,030 feet of altitude, scientists calculated that Austin's drive had to have an incredibly low launch angle and spin rate. They also calculated that Austin's swing speed would have had to have been at least 150 miles per hour to get the ball to carry 445 yards in the air before its roll. Austin's swing speed was once measured at 155 miles per hour.

"I KNEW I KNOCKED THE HELL OUT OF IT. BUT THE BALL WENT UP STRANGELY. WENT OUT ABOUT 10 OR 15 FEET HIGH AND KEPT GOING AND GOING AT THAT FLATTENED LEVEL. I COULD PUT MY FINGER ON IT THE WHOLE WAY BEFORE IT DROPPED."
—MIKE AUSTIN

#46 THE OLD COLLEGE TRY

OKLAHOMA'S CLASSIC WINNING STREAK SET THE STANDARD FOR BIG-TIME COLLEGE FOOTBALL

Head coach Bud Wilkinson (center, in hat) gathers his players for a huddle before a game on October 1, 1956, at the height of Oklahoma's 47-game winning streak. Photo courtesy of Time Life Pictures/Getty Images.

IT WOULD SEEM TO BE A NEAR-IMPOSSIBLE task: find a college football team and build a winning streak that lasts more than a couple of seasons. After all, in the pros, where teams don't have to worry about their stars graduating, the longest winning streak is 21 games, by the New England Patriots.

Yet college football has seen some remarkable runs. The two longest recent winning streaks among serious football schools are the 34-game streaks by Miami between 2000 and 2002, and USC from 2003 to 2005.

But both streaks had a bittersweet quality to them. Miami's run ended in a heartbreaking 31–24 upset loss to Ohio State in the Fiesta Bowl in double overtime. The Hurricanes thought they had won the National Championship in the first overtime, but a fourth-down pass interference call gave Ohio State new life. USC's skein ended in similar disappointment. They held a 12-point fourth-quarter lead against Texas, and a failed fourth-down conversion late in the game allowed Texas's Vince Young to get the ball back in good field position and scramble in for the winning score with only 19 seconds left on the clock.

Fans who can remember that far back have happier memories of the only major college streak to top those two, the 47-game streak put together by Bud Wilkinson's Oklahoma Sooners from 1953 through

TOUGH TO THE END

It's not as if Oklahoma's 47-game winning streak has really been challenged in the last half-century, and it's definitely not as if they went and gave it up during game number 48. Bud Wilkinson's two-time defending champion Sooners lost a 7–0 chess match to Notre Dame, with the only points being scored in the game's final five minutes.

1957. Oklahoma began that winning streak with a 19–14 victory over Texas on October 10, 1953. The last victory in the streak was a 39–14 win at Missouri on November 9, 1957. During that period they won back-to-back national championships in 1955 and 1956.

Wilkinson was no stranger to winning streaks—between 1948 and 1950 he led Oklahoma to a 31-game unbeaten streak. The even-tempered Wilkinson was not only one of the game's premier tacticians but also a master motivator. As Oklahoma prepared for its annual border battle with Texas in 1956, Wilkinson sensed that his team had not been very serious in practice. He walked into the locker room before the game to address the team.

"Gentlemen, I think that you know that you didn't practice well this week," he said in a calm and matter-of-fact manner. "But it is no disgrace to lose to a team such as Texas. Even so, when they beat you, just remember that you are still Oklahoma and keep your head held high." The team was shocked—and proceeded to go out and beat Texas 45–0.

Ironically, the end of the Sooner winning streak gave birth to one of sport's most enduring superstitions—the *Sports Illustrated* cover jinx. After the Sooners had reeled off win number 47 in a row, the magazine not only put the Sooners on the cover, but they also declared them the greatest college football team of all time. Less than a week later, the streak was over. The Sooners dropped a 7–0 decision to Notre Dame at home. Dick Lynch scored the only touchdown of the game for the Irish on a short run with less than four minutes to play.

After the loss to Notre Dame, Wilkinson didn't resort to histrionics. "Men," he told his players, "the only people who never lose are the ones who never play the game."

"GENTLEMEN, I THINK THAT YOU KNOW THAT YOU DIDN'T PRACTICE WELL THIS WEEK. BUT IT IS NO DISGRACE TO LOSE TO A TEAM SUCH AS TEXAS. EVEN SO, WHEN THEY BEAT YOU, JUST REMEMBER THAT YOU ARE STILL OKLAHOMA AND KEEP YOUR HEADS HELD HIGH."
—BUD WILKINSON, PRIOR TO THE SOONERS' 45–0 VICTORY OVER TEXAS IN 1956

ALL–TIME DIVISION I–A FOOTBALL WINNING STREAKS

1.	Oklahoma	47	1953–57
2.	Washington	39	1908–14
3. tie	Yale	37	1890–93
	Yale	37	1887–89
5.	Toledo	35	1969–71
6 tie	Pennsylvania	34	1894–96
	Miami (FL)	34	2000–02
	USC	34	2003–05
9. tie	Oklahoma	31	1948–50
	Pittsburgh	31	1914–18
	Pennsylvania	31	1896–98
12.	Texas	30	1968–70

USC's Lendale White (No. 21, at right), who was stopped short on a fourth-and-2 late in the fourth quarter of the 2006 Rose Bowl, watches Texas players celebrate on their way to a miraculous come-from-behind victory—ending the Trojans' formidable 34-game win streak.

#47 SHUT OUT THE LIGHT

FOR FIVE FLAWLESS GAMES, BRIAN BOUCHER WAS THE HOTTEST OF ALL GOALIES

Phoenix Coyotes goalie Brian Boucher makes the stop (puck can be seen in the center of his pads), with a little extra effort from Radoslav Suchy, defending against Washington's Peter Bondra, to help preserve Boucher's fourth-consecutive shutout on January 7, 2004.

DON'T BELIEVE IN THE HOT GOALIE

Theory? Then listen to the story of Brian Boucher. In February and March of 2004, the Phoenix Coyotes goalie won one game in 21 tries. A month earlier? He was impenetrable, having broken a 55-year-old record for the NHL's longest shutout streak.

Boucher's streak began on December 27, 2003, and lasted until January 11, 2004. For 332 minutes and one second, Boucher was perfect. He recorded five consecutive shutouts, becoming the first goalie to do that since the introduction of the red line in 1943–44.

On December 31, he recorded his first shutout as a Coyote, making 21 saves in the New Year's Eve affair. On January 2, Boucher extended his streak, earning his first road shutout since October 30, 2001, by stopping 35 Dallas shots. On January 4, Boucher ran the streak to 205:45, stopping 26 shots to shut out Carolina. On January 7, 2004, he became the first goalie in nearly 55 years to register four shutouts in a row. He blanked the Washington Capitals 3–0 at the MCI Center, saving all 27 shots in the win.

On January 9, 2004, Boucher had a date with destiny as the Coyotes faced the Minnesota Wild at the Xcel Energy Center. The modern shutout record was 309:21, set by legendary Canadien goalie Bill Durnan between February 24 and March 9, 1949. Early in the third period the record was Boucher's.

"I did look up at the clock," Boucher admitted. "Once I saw it was, I think, four minutes into the third, I knew I could breathe easy as far as the streak is concerned. That is probably the first time I really was counting down. I hate to do that, but I don't know if anyone could ignore it. I was happy that was over and then we could focus on just winning the game."

Boucher sealed the deal, stopping 21 shots on the night in a 2–0 victory. Perhaps his best save came against Richard Park, whose shot off a perfect pass from Sergei Zholtok ricocheted off Boucher's right pad.

"That's a goal 9.9 out of 10 times," Park said. "I got the shot off [that] I wanted, but it's remarkable the swagger he's got in the net, the confidence."

But just as that which goes up must come down, all hot goalies must cool off. On January 11, 2004, Boucher's record streak ended. At 6:16 of the first period, in Phoenix, Randy Robitaille fired a slap shot from the blue line which deflected off the chest of Phoenix defenseman David Tanabe and sailed past Boucher. "I don't think it would have hit the net if it didn't hit me," Tanabe said. "If it wasn't for that bounce, he could have had another shutout." Boucher, who made 21 saves in a 1–1 tie, was philosophical.

"A fluky goal," he said. "That's how easily a goal can go in. The fact that it didn't happen for five-plus games is pretty amazing."

Boucher was hardly a likely candidate to break a half-century-old record. At the beginning of the season, the Coyotes put him on waivers, and when he wasn't claimed, he was demoted to third-string goalie.

As impressive as Boucher's streak was, it was also a product of a new, lower-scoring NHL. Seven of the NHL's 10 longest shutout streaks were registered since 1998. And his brilliance, although very real, was fleeting. Over the last two months of the season, Boucher couldn't buy a win. "I've had my ups and downs and hockey is a strange game," he said. "Sometimes things happen that you really can't explain."

THE BATTERED BULLDOGS

The NHL record for the most goals in a game by one team is 16. The mark was set by the Montreal Canadiens, who trounced the Quebec Bulldogs 16–3 on March 3, 1920. The record for the most goals by a single player (7) was set by Joe Malone of the Quebec Bulldogs on January 31, 1920. And the record for points in a game by a single player (10) was set by Darryl Sittler of Toronto on February 7, 1976.

THE BIG OT

Which goalie came up biggest in the biggest of all situations? That would be Jean-Sebastien Giguere of the Anaheim Mighty Ducks. During the 2003 play-offs, the Montreal native set an NHL record by stonewalling opponents for 168 minutes and 27 seconds of sudden-death overtime in the playoffs. "There is no better way for me to get better as a player than being in overtime," Giguere said. "It doesn't get any better than that." The previous record of 162:56 belonged to Patrick Roy.

Bondra (No. 12) again finds himself, and the puck, being rejected from the goalmouth by Boucher and friends on the night of Boucher's 3–0 shutout that gave him four straight.

#48 GEEZER OF THE GRIDIRON

FOR MORE THAN A QUARTER OF A CENTURY, GEORGE BLANDA KICKED FIELD GOALS AND COMPLETED PASSES

HIS NAME IS RIGHT AT THE TOP OF THE first page of the NFL record book. In a sport where plenty of 26-year-old running backs are already retired, George Blanda played 26 years of professional football for the Chicago Bears, Baltimore Colts, Houston Oilers, and Oakland Raiders. His career, which started in 1949 and ended in 1975, spanned four decades.

Blanda is probably best remembered as a place-kicker, but he was not solely a special teamer. He played quarterback throughout his career, including into the 1970s, even after he was well past his 40th birthday. Indeed, some of the greatest success in Blanda's Hall of Fame career came in the later years. Perhaps his most memorable season came during the 1970 season, when he was 43.

It began on October 25, when he replaced an injured Daryle Lamonica and threw touchdown passes of 19, 43, and 44 yards in a 31–14 victory over Pittsburgh. The following week, he kicked a 48-yard field goal with three seconds left to give Oakland a 17–17 tie with Kansas City. On November 8, he replaced Lamonica in the fourth quarter with Oakland trailing by a touchdown. Blanda threw a 14-yard touchdown pass to tie the game with 1:14 remaining, then won it with a 52-yard field goal with three seconds to play. Against Denver on November 15, Blanda came in with

four minutes left and Oakland losing 19–17. He led an 80-yard drive, culminating in a 20-yard touchdown pass to Fred Biletnikoff for another victory. And on November 22, his 16-yard field goal with four seconds remaining gave Oakland a 20–17 win over San Diego. Thanks to Blanda's heroics, Oakland won the AFC Western Division championship and Blanda was named the AFC Player of the Year and the Associated Press Male Athlete of the Year.

Blanda played for two of football's most legendary coaches: Bear Bryant at Kentucky and George Halas with the Bears. However, neither of them was very impressed with Blanda's talents.

Bryant told Halas that he was getting an "average" player when he drafted him in 1949 and even though he lasted 10 years with the Bears, Halas didn't think all that much of Blanda.

"I never had much fun there," Blanda admitted. He had more fun with the Houston Oilers of the AFL, where he led the team to two titles and won Player of the Year honors in 1961. Blanda didn't have a great arm, but he managed to turn that weakness into a strength. He was a surprisingly effective passer, completing 1,911 of 4,007 passes for 26,920 yards and 236 touchdowns.

"Some quarterbacks you can anticipate," said former Raiders cornerback Dave Grayson. "They throw the ball about the same way every time. But not

George Blanda, at the age of 43, quarterbacked and kicked the Oakland Raiders into the playoffs and was named the AFC Player of the Year and the Associated Press Male Athlete of the Year.

"SOME QUARTERBACKS YOU CAN ANTICIPATE. THEY THROW THE BALL ABOUT THE
SAME WAY EVERY TIME. BUT NOT GEORGE. YOU CAN'T READ HIM.
ONE TIME HE'LL DRILL IT, THE NEXT TIME HE'LL LOFT IT A LITTLE, THEN HE'LL FLOAT IT."
—RAIDERS CORNERBACK DAVE GRAYSON

Blanda finished out his career as the Raiders' kicker and backup quarter-back. He usually found ways to win games at both positions.

"Age is a question of mind over matter. If you don't mind, it doesn't matter." That's the advice of the oldest major leaguer, Negro League legend Satchel Paige. The man whom Joe DiMaggio called "the best and fastest pitcher I've ever faced" was nearing his 60th birthday when he laced them up for the last time, partly as a publicity stunt masterminded by Kansas City A's owner Charlie Finley. On September 25, 1965, Paige got the last laugh when, at the age of 59, he threw three shutout innings.

The oldest hockey player is Gordie Howe. Mr. Hockey retired in the early 1970s but then returned so that he could play on the same team, the Detroit Red Wings, as sons Mark and Marty. Howe was 52 years old when he finally retired for good in 1980.

The oldest player in NBA history? It depends upon whom you ask. Robert Parish is often credited with this distinction, having played a record 1,611 games and retired as a member of the Chicago Bulls in 1997 at age 43. However, the Celtics legend was a mere pup compared to Nat Hickey, who stepped out onto the hardwood at age 46 for the Providence Steamrollers during the 1947–48 season. The 5'10" forward played in only one game and missed all six of his field-goal attempts.

George. You can't read him. One time he'll drill it, the next time he'll loft it a little, then he'll float it."

As a kicker, Blanda was one of the last of his breed, using a straight-on technique at a time when soccer-style kickers were taking over the NFL for good. Blanda kicked an NFL-record 943 extra points. He kicked 335 field goals and his 2,002 career points, including nine touchdowns that he scored, were a league record when he retired.

Blanda announced his retirement before the 1976 season, shortly before his 49th birthday making him the oldest player in league history. He was almost nine years younger than his coach, John Madden.

#49 AMAZINGLY BAD

THE 1962 METS SET A RECORD FOR LOSSES—AND INEPTITUDE

With ex-stars like Gil Hodges and Richie Ashburn and talents like Don Zimmer and Roger Craig, the 1962 Mets were widely believed to have been a better-than-average expansion team.

THE DEBATE OVER THE GREATEST BASEBALL team of all time isn't one that's easily settled. The 1927 Yankees? The 1931 A's? The 1939 Yankees?

But turn the tables—what's the worst team of all time?—and there's a consensus pick: the 1962 Mets. Now the 1899 Cleveland Spiders lost an even higher percentage of games, going 20–134. The 2003 Detroit Tigers set an AL record with their 43–119 mark. But the expansion Mets turned bad into an art form.

It's not so much that the Mets lost 120 games in 1962; it's how they lost. As the replacement for the Dodgers and Giants (hence their blue and orange colors), the expansion Mets carried a greater burden of expectation than most expansion teams. Add to that the presence of manager Casey Stengel—who only two years before had led the Yankees to the World Series—and former stars like Richie Ashburn and Gil Hodges, and you can see why optimistic fans might have thought that this team might have been at least decent.

Oh, boy, were they wrong. While the Mets won a dozen games in spring training, including a win over the defending champion New York Yankees, hopes were high, but the manager wasn't getting swept up in the hysteria. "I ain't fooled," Stengel told the beat writers. "They play different when the other team is trying,

Zimmer, a baseball lifer if ever there was one, has the distinction of making the first error for the famed—notorious, actually—1962 Mets.

too." The Old Professor was right, and the team started out 0–9.

The Mets lost in all the normal ways, and then they lost in ways that were truly unique. The first error was made by Charlie Neal, and Don Zimmer went hitless in 34 at-bats, at one point while batting only .077, before being traded to the Reds in May.

"That Zimmer's the guts of your club," a scout is said to have told Stengel.

"He's beyond that. He's the lower intestine," countered the voluble Stengel.

The first run in franchise history was allowed by Roger Craig, who would go on to lose 24 games that year. A popular urban legend says he simply dropped the ball during his windup, balking home a runner on third. The Mets' first-ever win came in their 10th game against the previously undefeated Pittsburgh Pirates, and the winning pitcher was Jay Hook, a Northwestern grad who was described by Casey as "the world's smartest pitcher until he takes the mound."

Wins would be few and far between that year, and the team's best month of that lost season came in May, when the Mets won nine games and lost 17.

But the stories of that season have endured for as long as the team's record of futility has. In one of the classic tales of that season, first baseman Marvelous Marv Throneberry, who became a symbol of that team's ineptitude, hit a triple but was called out for failing to tag second base. When Stengel came out to argue with the umpire, he was admonished, "Don't argue too hard, Casey. He missed first, too."

"Well, I know he touched third because he's standing right on it," Stengel is said to have replied.

The team wouldn't have a winning month until July 1966, after Stengel's departure and after the loveable losers shtick had become less endearing.

A 1964 joke had a beat writer calling in to his editor from a windy Wrigley Field. Writer: "The Mets scored 19 runs today."

Editor: "But did they win?"

The 1962 Mets ended their season much as they had started it, with a 5–1 loss to the Cubs, their 120th of the year. But still the Amazings ended their inaugural season just as their leader had predicted. "Where's the team going to finish, Casey?" reporters asked him in spring training.

"We're going to finish in Chicago," he replied.

Center fielder Richie Ashburn went so far as to learn "I got it" in Spanish to offset the comedy of errors taking place in the Mets' outfield, but to no avail.

NATIONAL LEAGUE SCOUT: "THAT ZIMMER'S THE GUTS OF YOUR CLUB."

CASEY STENGEL: "HE'S BEYOND THAT. HE'S THE LOWER INTESTINE."

THEY GOT IT

The 1962 Mets became a piece of music history when the indie band Yo La Tengo, led by Georgia Hubley and Ira Kaplan, took their name from a famous incident in that first season.

Richie Ashburn, the future Hall of Fame center fielder, had communication problems with Venezuelan shortstop Elio Chacon. When Ashburn came in for a catch, he would shout, "I got it! I got it!" but Chacon, who spoke only Spanish, kept coming and they would collide. Ashburn found a bilingual teammate who told him to yell "Yo la tengo," or "I got it" in Spanish.

The next game, Ashburn and Chacon thought they had it resolved. Another short pop fly, and Ashburn yelled "Yo la tengo!" Chacon stopped in his tracks. And just as he was about to catch the ball, Ashburn was then flattened by left fielder Frank Thomas, who spoke no Spanish.

#50

PERFECT ATTENDANCE

CAL RIPKEN DIDN'T TAKE A DAY OFF FOR 15 YEARS— BUT WAS THAT A GOOD THING?

Baltimore's Cal Ripken acknowledges the crowd as the sign in center field reads 2,131, signifying his breaking of Lou Gehrig's record of playing in 2,130 consecutive games.

THEY SAID IT COULDN'T BE BROKEN, OR so almost everyone thought. But day after day, season after season, Cal Ripken Jr. of the Baltimore Orioles just kept showing up for work. And finally on September 6, 1995, Ripken played in his 2,131st consecutive game, one more than Lou Gehrig's legendary mark.

What the it'll-stand-forever contingent didn't consider is that given the right circumstances—a player who's good enough to stay in the lineup every day for 15 years and who is lucky enough to avoid serious injury—a consecutive-games streak is more a function of will than skill. In that way it's less like hitting in 57 consecutive games—every batter tries to get a hit every time up but no one does—and more like spending a career without ever stepping on the third-base line. If you really want it badly enough you probably can. After all, Gehrig presumably got the idea for his streak from watching his teammate Everett Scott set the endurance record that Gehrig eventually broke.

The biggest clue that Gehrig's record was vulnerable was the fact that it had been broken once, before Ripken even got close. In 1987, Sachio Kinugasa of the Hiroshima Carp surpassed Gehrig and went on to play in 2,215 consecutive games. But Ripken claimed the world record on June 14, 1996.

Ripken continued his streak, stretching it to 2,632 games before finally bowing out of the lineup on

THE RIPKEN EFFECT

During Ripken's streak, the Orioles were 1,334–1,297. Ripken was replaced in 130 games during that time. He batted .277 during the streak, and he played for seven managers, including Earl Weaver, who began on May 30, 1982, and Ray Miller, who managed the game on which the streak ended on September 20, 1998. During the streak the Orioles finished first in the AL East twice (1983 and 1997) and lost 95 or more games three times.

Ripken gets another ovation from fans during his record-tying 2,130th consecutive game, this on the previous night of September 5, 1995, in Baltimore.

September 19, 1998, against the Yankees. "I think the time is right," he told manager Ray Miller before sitting out his first game since May 30, 1982.

While Ripken's consecutive-games streak is impressive at some level, it's also likely that in putting his pursuit of a record ahead of the rest of his game, Ripken actually hurt his team. In his sophomore season, Ripken won the MVP award and helped the Orioles to the World Championship, hitting .318 with 27 homers.

How many times did he reach either of those two relatively modest milestones over the next 18 seasons? Exactly once. How many subsequent trips to the Fall Classic? None. He scored 100 runs three times by the age of 24, and not once afterwards. He drove in 100 runs twice by age 24, and only twice thereafter. Whereas most Major League careers resemble a bell curve, with a long period of increasing productivity, Ripken's is more like a ski slope, a gradual inexorable decline, with one single bump in his other MVP year of 1991. (For the record, Lou Gehrig—who played shorter seasons and sometimes left the game after only one at-bat— followed a more normal pattern, and his hitting stats rank him as arguably the greatest first baseman of all time.)

That's an awful lot to sacrifice for what's essentially a perfect attendance record. It's hard not to think that Ripken—and the Orioles— would have been better off if he had taken a day off now and then.

As to the question of whether Ripken's record is unbreakable, even the man who set it is under no illusions. "A lot of people think this is a great, great accomplishment," Ripken said. "But I really believe that somebody else will come along and play more games, because if I can do it, somebody else definitely will."

THE OTHER IRONMEN

Because of baseball's everyday nature, the longest consecutive-games streaks in other sports are less than half as long as Ripken's.

NBA   A. C. Green, 1,192 games

NHL   Doug Jarvis, 964 games

NFL   Jeff Feagles, 288 games

The Iron Horse, Lou Gehrig, takes a rare breather to watch his Yankees teammates warm up before a game in 1939.

"A LOT OF PEOPLE THINK THIS IS A GREAT, GREAT ACCOMPLISHMENT.
BUT I REALLY BELIEVE THAT SOMEBODY ELSE WILL COME ALONG AND
PLAY MORE GAMES, BECAUSE IF I CAN DO IT, SOMEBODY ELSE DEFINITELY WILL."
—CAL RIPKEN JR.